ParaReading

A Training Guide for Tutors

THE GIFT OF LEARNING TO READ

→ When we teach a child to read, we change his/her life's trajectory.

Deborah R. Glaser, Ed.D.

BOSTON, MA • NEW YORK, NY • LONGMONT, CO

A LETRS Supplement Module

Language Essentials for Teachers of Reading and Spelling

09 08 07 06 4 5 6 7 8 9

ISBN 1-59318-399-2

Printed in the United States of America

Published and Distributed by

Sopris West™
EDUCATIONAL SERVICES

A Cambium Learning Company

4093 Specialty Place • Longmont, Colorado 80504 • (303) 651-2829
www.sopriswest.com

109671/10-05

Acknowledgments

For several of my teaching years, I was fortunate to have paraeducators at my side, working with me and assisting me with my teaching and the multiple daily tasks teachers face. I learned numerous lessons from these generous and caring individuals. One of those lessons was that if I taught *them* well, these successful paraeducators ended up leaving me and returning to college to get their teaching certificates! It was always difficult to say goodbye, but these were joyous occasions too, because these individuals had experienced the positive results of appropriately designed reading instruction with their students. They were proof that knowledgeable, well-trained tutors can make a difference in young children's reading skills.

Paraeducators deserve training that incorporates current scientifically based research to help them be the strongest reading tutors they can be. Students deserve to learn from tutors who understand the reading process and what and how to teach, so that not a moment is lost in becoming a reader. I wish the many paraeducators who complete this training countless joyful successes in the work they do with young children and in their collaborative efforts with classroom teachers.

Louisa Moats and Steve Mitchell of Sopris West are stars in my life. I thank them for recognizing the critical need for qualified paraeducators and for giving me the opportunity to produce this training guide. Thank you for being my teacher, Louisa; I never fail to learn something new from you. And thank you Holly Bell at Sopris West for being the cheerleader who encouraged and supported my efforts throughout!

About the Author

Deborah Glaser, Ed.D., is an educational consultant and trainer based in Boise, Idaho. She brings 28 years of teaching experience to her current work with schools, teachers, and reading program development. Deborah wrote the *Comprehensive Literacy Plan* on which Idaho's Reading Initiative was based, and she has trained thousands of teachers across the country on the foundations of learning to read and how to teach reading effectively so that *all* children learn. She is a national trainer for *Language Essentials for Teachers of Reading and Spelling* (*LETRS*) and *Dynamic Indicators of Basic Early Literacy Skills* (*DIBELS*). *ParaReading* was developed to assist with filling the need for qualified tutors who understand the underlying reading skills young children need and how to teach them. Her professional interests include building professional learning communities through collaboration, with a focus on improving reading skills for all children, and evaluating professional development in ways that reflect teacher learning and student achievement.

Contents

Introduction

A Need for Trained Reading Tutors

The demand for well-informed, trained, and knowledgeable educators and paraeducators[1] is greater than it has ever been. Paraeducators play a critical and significant role in schools and learning centers as a support to the teaching and learning process. Current statistics from the U.S. Department of Education reveal that, in 87% of Title 1 schools, paraeducators are assigned the responsibility of teaching reading (U.S. Department of Education, 1999). This dependence on paraeducators demands the attention of teachers, school administrators, and parents. Have we prepared our paraeducators to implement proven teaching practices that will promote successful levels of student achievement and reading ability? Schools are increasingly responsive to calls for scientific, research-based reading instruction. It is important that all reading instructors, including paraeducators, know how young children learn to read and that they are trained in how to implement best practices to ensure that *all* children become readers.

Legislation under the No Child Left Behind Act (2001) addresses the paraeducators' role and requires that they receive training to support the application of scientifically researched principles of reading instruction. Research with trained paraeducators demonstrates that the educational community can have high expectations for the paraeducator as reading tutor. Trained paraeducators using a structured program can be as effective as experts with advanced degrees (Elbaum, Vaughn, Hughes, & Moody, 2000; Vadasy, Jenkins, & Pool, 2000). These findings intensify the need for paraeducator training that addresses the core reading components and provides the essential knowledge of both *what* to teach and *how* to teach reading to young children.

ParaReading provides thoughtful and well-designed materials for formal paraeducator training. This training ensures that tutors are indeed qualified to implement structured reading programs and to assist teachers with the instruction of students who are at risk in reading and spelling. *ParaReading* offers the crucial training to enrich, strengthen, and build a resource for sustainable and strategic instruction, so that all children learn to read.

[1] The term "paraeducator" was purposefully chosen for this publication because it describes most clearly the role of paraprofessional, volunteer, tutor, and classroom assistant. *Paraeducator* references a level of expertise in the education field in the same way that *paralegal* does in the field of law.

Basis for ParaReading Content

ParaReading bases its curriculum on the National Reading Panel's key instructional recommendations (Report of the National Reading Panel, 2000). These key reading skill components—phonemic awareness, decoding (or phonics), fluency, vocabulary, and comprehension—are presented within an instructional design that establishes a strong base for knowledge, application, and implementation of these five comprehensive reading program elements. Supplementary training is also included in maintaining records of students' performance, handling student errors effectively, and communicating with supervisors. A knowledgeable paraeducator has the potential to strengthen any elementary classroom's reading program.

The Paraeducator's Workbook and the Trainer's Manual

ParaReading contains the materials necessary to train paraeducators. The front section is a workbook for the paraeducator. The trainer's section in the back mirrors the workbook page numbers and adds pertinent training procedures and script. The training can be delivered using a number of schedule options to meet the needs of schools, districts, and individuals involved. Recommendations include:

- Training one component at a time. Allow approximately three hours per component for a relaxed training atmosphere with thorough material coverage.
- Training over two full days. Allow approximately six hours per day. The material can be covered adequately in this time period; however, consider offering a follow-up at a later date to review and strengthen the material and to cover the information in the Tutor's Tips section.
- Customizing the training to meet predetermined needs or to address weak component areas. If schools choose this option, we recommend that the Phonemic Awareness and Phonics sections be offered in the order presented and that neither one be omitted from the training.

Trainer Qualifications

ParaReading was created with the intent that local reading specialists, curriculum directors, and other individuals who have completed *Language Essentials for Teachers of Reading and Spelling* (Moats, 2003) or other in-depth and current reading professional development programs would be able to provide the *ParaReading* training. It is imperative that all *ParaReading* trainers:

- Understand the contributing role of oral language to reading development.
- Possess thorough instructional knowledge of the five reading components.
- Have worked with children using a structured and systematic comprehensive reading program.
- Understand the work that is asked of paraeducators.
- Be recognized as effective, efficient educators.

Community colleges and universities will find *ParaReading* to be an explicit and complete teaching tool for use in their paraeducator training programs.

Preparing to Implement ParaReading

We recommend that trainers use the following process to prepare for *ParaReading*. (In-depth directions for using the program are outlined in the Trainer's Manual.)

1. Preview the Paraeducator's Workbook lessons to get a sense of each chapter's organization. Read the workbook carefully, and then read the trainer's text in the Trainer's Manual; it provides step-by-step instructions for teaching the content. Highlight main ideas and details in the trainer's text for easy reference during the training.
2. Complete the Paraeducator's Workbook prior to teaching it. This will provide you with hands-on experience with the tasks that will be asked of the participants.
3. Make overhead transparencies from the blackline masters provided at the end of *ParaReading*. Place them in protector sheets in a notebook organized by component for use during training.

4. Gather and prepare the activity materials. Necessary workshop and training materials for each chapter are listed near the beginning of the Trainer's Manual.

5. Prepare to assess the participants' knowledge after each component. Answer this question: What will the process be for reassessment if a paraeducator does not meet criteria of 90% to 100% accuracy? Recommendations: Paraeducator (a) attends another training session; (b) is observed while tutoring and provided with feedback and modeling as necessary and then reassessed; or (c) is provided private, one-on-one or small group review of the information, followed by reassessment.

Research Base for ParaReading

Research utilizing twelve single-case studies highlights the instructional effectiveness of paraeducators trained in the foundation of how young children learn to read and how to apply specific instructional methods (Glaser, 2002). High school senior tutors completed explicit background training and applied a systematic four-step lesson teaching three of the five research-based components: phonemic awareness, decoding, and fluency.

Each tutor worked with two different students for six weeks. Oral reading fluency measures were gathered (Edformation, 2002) every two weeks for twelve weeks throughout this experiment. Baseline, treatment, and post-treatment data were compared using a statistical method determined to be sensitive to individual changes across outcome measures when moderately few data points are available (Mueser, Yarnold, & Foy, 1991). Five students demonstrated significant gains in reading fluency, and additional analysis revealed that all students (N = 12) made increases, averaging 2.5 words per week, in words read per minute. These findings are comparable to a similar, seven-week study utilizing certified classroom and special education teachers (Hasbrouk, Ihnot, & Rogers, 1999), where students made between a 1.23 and 2.35 words-per-week gain.

These and other studies demonstrate that trained, noncertified tutors can improve reading fluency (Elbaum et al., 2000). Gains in reading fluency, measured by words read correct per minute, have been highly correlated with improved comprehension (Shinn, Deno, & Fuchs, 2002); fluency gains match up with overall reading gains. By placing *trained* paraeducators with students at risk of reading failure, schools increase opportunities for successful tutoring experiences where students improve reading skills and bolster their self-esteem and confidence in their abilities. Schools

that utilize *trained* tutors to support classroom teachers' instruction increase the chances for students to learn in small groups where the learning and the instructional pace can be monitored for greater gains.

The educational community is increasing its use of paraeducators to tutor greater numbers of students who are at risk and low performing in reading (Cohen, Kulik, & Kulik, 1982). Paraeducators make a vital contribution to successful reading programs, but key to their success is intentional training in the process of how children learn to read and how to implement proven teaching practices. *ParaReading* provides core training intended to improve the efforts of reading tutors and the abilities of the children they teach.

The Paraeducator's Workbook

Welcome to the Paraeducator

Welcome to *ParaReading*. This paraeducator training will prepare you to be a confident, knowledgeable reading tutor who is available to help children, their families, and the personnel with whom you work. Children benefit from the relationships you build with them because students who work one on one with caring tutors demonstrate improved self-esteem and confidence (Wasik, 1998; Fitzgerald, 2001). Families profit when their children who are at risk of academic failure begin to succeed and gain confidence as learners. And schools and learning centers need paraeducators to provide the needed manpower to reach all children. As a paraeducator, you are a very valuable person and perform a very important role. The goals (broad-based learning) and objectives (action-oriented, observable outcomes) for your *ParaReading* training are listed below.

Goals

Effective paraeducators:

- Understand the important roles that phonemic awareness, phonics (or decoding), fluency, vocabulary, and comprehension have in reading instruction.
- Learn how to apply systematic and direct practices to teach students the five basic components of reading.
- Acquire specific instructional, record-keeping, and tutorial management skills.

Objectives

Effective paraeducators:

- Observe modeling of instructional techniques and instructional content and participate in role-playing during the training.
- Demonstrate mastery of the explicit systematic learning that strengthens effective reading instruction.
- Deliver praise, encouragement, positive feedback, and reinforcement as part of their successful instruction.

- Recognize areas in which students need extra help, and understand the importance of communicating observations to supervisors when there are questions or concerns.
- Utilize error-correction procedures that are quick, simple, and consistently applied.
- Keep accurate records as an assessment of a student's progress, of their work, and for program evaluation.

ParaReading Training

Content

ParaReading training is based upon five critical components of reading instruction. These components can be illustrated as five points on a star:

Integrated, Comprehensive Reading Instruction

1 Phonemic Awareness

2 Phonics

3 Fluency

4 Vocabulary

5 Comprehension

To further strengthen your training, suggestions for data collection, organization, how to respond to student errors, and communication with supervising teachers are included in the Tutor's Tips section of this workbook, along with additional instructional advice. In the Tutor's Tips section, you will also find Strategy Reference Cards, the tutor strategies that you learn in this training formatted for use as a quick teaching reference!

Format

The Paraeducator's Workbook presents each of the five reading components in its own chapter designed to help you become familiar with the component and how to teach it. Your lessons will follow this consistent format:

- **Discussion**—Each chapter begins with a discussion of the focus component. Your trainer will present background information and research, so that you will understand the importance of the skill being taught.
- **Your Turn to Learn**—Your Turn to Learn provides opportunities for you to practice and perfect your own reading skills in the area of focus. Paraeducators may have their skills assessed during this section.
- **How to Teach It**—Procedures for teaching the focus skill are presented in this section. Necessary instructional materials are listed, and a data collection process is described.
- **Practice It**—Before you teach any reading skill, you should have lots of practice! The training allows time to observe, practice in pairs, and role-play with other tutors and the trainer.
- **Review**—A brief review assessment completes each chapter. These reviews are meant to provide helpful feedback to you and your trainer as you progress through the training.

Note to the Paraeducator When we teach, it is natural to assume that our students will learn using the same methods and tools that *our* teachers used when we were learning. It is important to put aside your memories of how you learned and even how your own children learned as you begin this training. Research provides the key to helping us design and deliver instruction that works for the majority of kids at risk (Foorman, Francis, Fletcher, Schatschneider, & Mehta 1998; Moats, 1999). *ParaReading* uses this research as the basis for training you to implement effective, proven reading practices. Good luck! You are on your way to becoming a *ParaReading* tutor and to giving the gift of reading to the children you teach!

Before We Begin

Exercise

Consider your previous encounters with a child who had difficulty learning to read. Who comes to mind? A boy or a girl? How old? What were some of this child's experiences with learning to read?

Use colored markers and a piece of paper to draw the person you're thinking of. It doesn't have to be a work of art ready to hang in a museum; the critical thing here is that you create an image of the person who will represent why you want to learn how to effectively help children improve their reading.

Write about your person:

1. Tell about why you chose this person.
2. Tell about an event you recall that illustrates the difficulty this person had with learning to read.

Karen	Andrea
-Unable to decipher word	Same
- letter sounds	word chunking
- language difficulty	comprehension
	predicting
	inferences

Post your drawing in an area of the room set aside by your trainer. Look at all of the pictures of all of the children. Imagine that they are your students while you learn *ParaReading*!

Chapter 1: Phonemic Awareness

Discussion

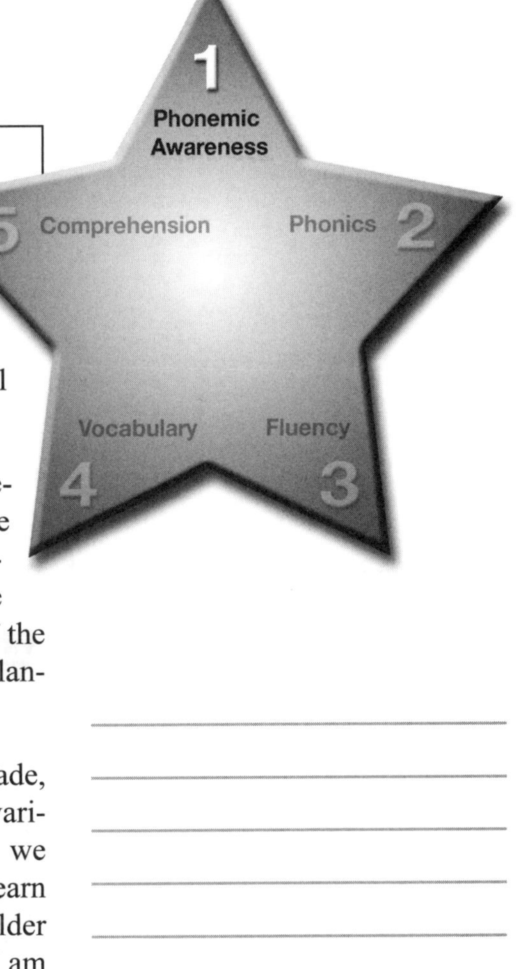

Exercise #1: Listen and respond as your trainer asks you to answer some simple word-play tasks.

The tasks that you just completed require a linguistic skill called *phonemic awareness*. Phonemic awareness happens in the absence of visual letters. The listener's focus is on oral language, on speech sounds.

The ability to separate and produce speech sounds in words requires one to have phonemic awareness, or awareness of the speech sounds in one's own language. This ability seems simple to us, yet to many young children the questions you were asked are not easy to answer. Phonemic awareness is one of the critical skills that enable young children to decode written language into spoken language and read!

If you ask a young child who is preparing to enter first grade, "What are you going to learn in school?", the answer will invariably be, "I am going to learn to read!" First grade is where we gain entrance into the world of reading. School is where we learn to read. Reading is what opens worlds to us; reading is what older brothers and sisters, friends, and parents can do, and, now, "I am going to learn to read too!"

Unfortunately, though, reading does not come easily to about 40% of children (Vellutino & Scanlon, 1987). They watch anxiously as others in their class begin to make sense of those letters on a page, while it remains a struggle to them. Slowly, over time, if they do not "catch on," these struggling children become frustrated; confidence is lost, and they feel "dumb." In fact, most of these children simply lack a skill that can be taught to them: *phonemic awareness*!

A few years ago, children showed up on the first day of school and teachers would show them the letter "A" and instruct, "This letter says /a/ as in *apple*." Educators assumed something very critical to the process of reading. They assumed that children were able to conceptualize the individual sounds of their language and isolate individual sounds from the other sounds in a word. Educators have learned that many children—two out of five—are not able to do this when they enter first grade and many who continue to make

slow progress in reading persist with low levels of speech-sound awareness. Without this ability to identify sounds and to separate and blend speech sounds within their language, children have serious difficulty with decoding and, consequently, learning to read.

Phonemes are the basic building blocks of spoken language. They are the separate speech sounds that, when combined in seamless streams, create the language we so effortlessly use to communicate. The awareness that speech is composed of sounds that can be isolated from each other has proven to be one of the most fundamental skills for young readers to possess.

> **Tutors Know!** *Phoneme*: a speech sound. Phonemic awareness allows one to identify the speech sounds in words. Examples: "There are three speech sounds in house—/h/ /ow/ /s/." "The last sound in book is /k/."

Your Turn to Learn

When you teach young children to read, it is important to be able to understand and sympathize with what they are experiencing. You are a reader. This makes it a challenge to understand students' experiences as they learn to read or work to improve their reading skills. It is critical to recognize that many of the students with whom you will work do not yet have a concept of the individual sounds, the *phonemes*, that make up the words that they read and speak. They have not yet developed phonemic awareness, and this may make learning to read difficult.

Your own phonemic awareness may not be as well developed as it needs to be to teach reading to young and struggling readers. Many adults need practice. This section will prepare you to include phoneme instruction in your lessons by building your *personal* understanding of phonemic awareness.

> **Tutors Know!** When you see a letter inside of two marks, like /m/, you say the sound represented by the letter, not the letter name.

What Phonemic Awareness Is

Phonemes are the individual sounds that combine to create the language we speak. For example, the sounds /t/, /ă/, and /k/ are separate sounds that we create with our tongues, teeth, and throats, and they can be arranged in a certain order to create the word *cat*. There are 43 different phonemes in the English language. Every language has a unique set of phonemes.

The following chart presents the 43 phonemes and examples of the sounds in words. The phonemes are divided into consonant sounds and vowel sounds. Practice saying these sounds with your trainer. When you say the sounds, be very careful not to add an additional separate sound, /ŭ/, to these sounds. Say /b/, not /buh/. Notice these characteristics when you practice saying the sounds:

- Feel your throat as you say each consonant sound. Do you feel a vibration? Is the sound a "voiced" sound or an "unvoiced" sound? Be careful! You will discover that there are sounds you may be voicing when in fact they are voiceless!
- Use a mirror. What is your tongue doing when you say the sounds? Is it tapping somewhere in your mouth? Is it flattened? In the back of your mouth or in the front?
- Which sounds share similar articulation features?

Consonant Sounds			Vowel Sounds		
1.	/b/	butter	26.	/e/	see
2.	/p/	pet	27.	/ĭ/	sit
3.	/m/	mouse	28.	/a/	make
4.	/f/	fuzz	29.	/ĕ/	bed
5.	/v/	vest	30.	/ă/	cat
6.	/th/	think	31.	/i/	time
7.	/th/	them	32.	/ŏ/	fox
8.	/t/	tiger	33.	/ŭ/	cup
9.	/d/	desk	34.	/aw/	saw, call, water, bought
10.	/n/	nose	35.	/o/	vote
11.	/s/	smile	36.	/oo/	book
12.	/z/	zipper	37.	/u/	tube, moo
13.	/sh/	ship	38.	/ə/ (schwa)	about, lesson
14.	/zh/	measure	39.	/oi/	oil, boy
15.	/ch/	chair	40.	/ou/	out, cow
16.	/j/	judge	41.	/er/	her, fur, sir
17.	/k/	kite	42.	/ar/	car
18.	/g/	goat	43.	/or/	corn
19.	/ng/	sang			
20.	/y/	yellow			
21.	/wh/	whistle			
22.	/w/	wagon			
23.	/h/	hand			
24.	/l/	lion			
25.	/r/	rose			

Exercise #2: Practice saying these sounds with a partner and for your trainer.

Turn to the LETRS consonant and vowel articulation charts in the back of your workbook. Now, practice saying the sounds again using these charts as a reference.

Tricky sounds abound when we start isolating them from the whole words we speak. These are a few that you will need to know because you are sure to run into them with your students. What is the surprise in each of these?

—chicken letter = always needs "u" for word

Quilt = /k/ /w/ /i/ /l/ /t/

Box = /b/ /o/ /k/ /s/

Universe = /y/ /oo/ /n/ /ə/ /v/ /r/ /s/

Phonemic awareness is the awareness that our speech is made up of separate sounds. Phonemic awareness enables children to isolate the first sound, last sound, and middle sounds when they hear or say a word. It allows them to separate out all the phonemes in words and to match them to written symbols. *To think phonemically, is to consider the spoken sound separately from the letter we use to represent the sound in our written language.* This is difficult for adults who are readers! We automatically visualize letters in our minds when we hear speech sounds. Young readers must learn to match phoneme sequences to letter patterns. For many, the process of reading falls apart at the basic level of phonemic awareness.

Exercise #3: Review and Discuss

Turn to your partner, and ask and answer these questions: What is a phoneme? What is phonemic awareness? Why is phonemic awareness important for young children to have?

Work together to write your answers here.

Exercise #4: Test and Practice Your Phonemic Awareness

Do the following Phonemic Awareness Activities with your trainer.

Phoneme Matching

Read the first word in each line and isolate the sound that is represented by the underlined letter or letter cluster. Then select the word or words in the line that contain the same sound. Circle the words you select.

1.	**hook**	food	cloud	foot	sugar
2.	**laugh**	faun	train	sauce	grand
3.	**miss**	does	nose	box	close
4.	**cage**	gym	game	gnat	hang
5.	**think**	blunt	sling	drink	hang

Count the Phonemes

Count the number of phonemes in the following words: f-o-k-s

through	3	loose	3	fox	~~3~~ 4	knight	3
high	2	pitcher	4	judge	3	fir	2
pay	2	torch	3	strong (s-t-r-o-ng)	~~3~~ 5	oil	2
wheat	3	quiet	4	vision	~~3~~ 5	cream	~~3~~ 4

v-i-zh-i-on c-r-e-m

Identification of Phonemes

Identify the third phoneme in the following words: s-k-w

shoes	~~s~~ z	square	~~r~~ w	notched	ch
night	t	vision	zh	square	~~ø~~ w
sing	ng	odor	r	walk	k

(continued) **Exercise #4:** Test and Practice Your Phonemic Awareness

Now, pair up with someone and do the following phoneme tasks with your partner.

Isolating Phonemes—Think of three additional words that have the same sound as the underlined letter or letters in each word. List them. Be ready to share your collections of words!

itch	witch, hitch, switch
thought	fought, robot, caught
tree	free, creep, relief
boy	oil, toil, coy
bird	heard, curd, absurd

Segmenting Phonemes—Segment and count the phonemes for each of the following words. Place a penny or other marker in each of the squares to represent each sound in the word. Record the number of sounds.

tap to the left

house	3	h	ow	s	(slide)			
friend	5	f/r	ĕ	n	d			
shelf	4	sh	e	l	f			
thought	3	th	ŏ	t				
key	2	k	ē					
youth	3	y	oo	th				
fox	4	f	ŏ	k	s			
knock	3	n	ŏ	k				
scrunched	7	s	k	r	u	n	ch	d

(continued) **Exercise #4:** Test and Practice Your Phonemic Awareness

Note: The previous activity is commonly used to teach segmentation to young children. When teaching young children to segment, it is important to use one box for each sound in the words they segment.

Auditory Blending—Take turns with your partner and say the given word separated out into all of its individual sounds. Leave about one second between each sound and then ask your partner to identify the word. Do not look at the word if you are the partner who is listening!

Partner One: Separate the Sounds		Partner Two: Separate the Sounds	
Growth	/g/ /r/ /oe/ /th/	Swish	/s/ /w/ /i/ /sh/
Axe	/a/ /k/ /s/	Touch	/t/ /u/ /ch/
Swoop	/s/ /w/ /oo/ /p/	Phone	/f/ /oe/ /n/
Pitch	/p/ /i/ /ch/	Quick	/k/ /w/ /i/ /k/
Think	/th/ /i/ /ng/ /k/	Drum	/d/ /r/ /u/ /m/
Brook	/b/ /r/ /oo/ /k/	Chalk	/ch/ /o/ /k/

How to Teach It: Phonemic Awareness

By including purposeful attention to phonemes when you tutor struggling readers, you are building a base that they will use to improve decoding and spelling. Prepare to include phonemic awareness in your lessons by using the advice in this section!

You will not do *all* of the following activities with your students in one lesson, but do spend about four minutes of your instructional time specifically on teaching phonemic awareness.

Choose Your Words Carefully

When you prepare to teach phonemic awareness, it is critical to consider and carefully choose the words you use. If your reading program provides lists of words for phoneme exercises, then you're set to go! If not, you will need to know how to match the words you choose with your students' phoneme ability level. Here are suggestions and examples of word choices that demonstrate an order of difficulty from simple to more complex.

1. Choose single-syllable words. The words provided by your school's reading program for reading practice are often the best to use for phonemic awareness activities too! Examples: *fan*, *pick*, *be*.

2. Use words beginning with continuant sounds for beginners. Examples /m/ and /s/.

3. If your student is beginning to isolate first and ending sounds, begin with words that have two or three sounds. For isolating middle sounds, make sure that your word choices are three-sound words. Examples: *cut*, *dirt*, *bead*.

4. Consonant digraphs (/th/, /sh/, etc.) represent one phoneme and are easily separated within words by early readers. Examples: *with*, *shot*, *chip*.

5. Avoid beginning- and ending-consonant blends until students can segment and blend words without blends. Then start with simple beginning two-sound blends. Examples: *blow*, *crutch*, *grace*. When students can segment beginning blends, use words with ending blends. Examples: *wind*, *milk*, *bent*.

6. Short and long vowel sounds are easier to segment than the vowel teams (/ă/ is easier than /ow/). Examples: *dot*, *doze* as opposed to *shout*, *foil*.

Exercise #5

Place these words in order of simple to complex using the headings provided. Provide another example word for each item.

waist flap at graft chief shift

fact night moist pup broil froze swift

2 or 3 Sounds	Initial Blends	Ending Blends	Initial and Ending Blends	Vowel Diphthongs

Multisensory Instruction

Multisensory instruction means that students simultaneously see, hear, and touch what they are learning. Teach your students the following multisensory cues to get them involved and to make it fun!

Multisensory Cues

- *Tap the Sounds*—Beginning with your index finger, tap once for each sound as you move through each finger.
- *Tap Head, Waist, Ankles*—To help students isolate middle sounds, use three-sound words and tap your head for the first sound, your waist for the middle sound, and then reach down to your feet for the last sound.
- *Finger Count*—Count and say the sounds one at a time, raising a finger for each sound.

- ***Pull the Sounds Out of Your Mouth***—Starting at your lips, pretend to grasp each isolated sound as you move your thumb and forefinger in a pulling movement away from your mouth.

- ***Use Manipulatives***—Little crackers, paper squares, or game pieces make good visuals that can help young children see the segmentation as they separate the sounds in words.

Word Play—A Developmental Continuum

When teaching phonemic awareness, engage the child in *word play*. Phonemic awareness is developed along a continuum. Children initially learn to isolate first sounds in words, then ending sounds, and so on. Practice each of these with your trainer using your multisensory cues.

- ***Isolate First Sounds***—Say the word and ask student to say the word and the first sound in that word. Repeat the word and sound with the student.

  Example: You say, "House." Student says, "House, /h/." Together, you say, "House, /h/."

- ***Isolate Last Sounds***—Say the word and ask the student to say the word and the last sound in that word. Repeat the word and the sound with the student.

  Example: You say, "Jump." Student says, "Jump, /p/." Together, you say, "Jump, /p/."

- ***Isolate Middle Sounds***—Say the word and ask the student to say the word and the middle sound in that word. Repeat the word and the sound with the student. Three-sound words work best.

  Example: You say, "Wave." Student says, "Wave, /ae/." Together, you say, "Wave, /ae/."

- ***Segment All Sounds in a Word***—Say a word and ask the student to tell you all of the little sounds in that word.

  Example: You say, "House." Student says, "House, /h/, /ou/, /s/." Together, you say, "House, /h/, /ou/, /s/."

- ***Auditory Blending ("Secret" Language)***—Say a word segmented into its isolated sounds, and ask the student to say the "secret word" back to you.

  Example: You say, "/l/ /ee/ /f/." Student says, "Leaf."

Tutors Know! *Complete Segmentation:* Separating all of the little sounds in a word—bead = /b//ee//d/. *Auditory Blending:* Blending the sounds of segmented word back into the whole word—/w//r//k/ = work!

Error Response

It is important to respond to students' errors in ways that will validate their efforts and draw attention to their errors as you correct them. Immediate feedback and correction will provide opportunities to increase learning.

1. Point out one thing that was done correctly. "Yes, the last sound is /t/."
2. Demonstrate the correct way. "Watch while I say all of the little sounds in the word: /m/ /ă/ /t/."
3. Point out the place where a correction was made. "There are two different sounds here, /m/ and /ă/, not one."
4. Student does it again with you. "Do it with me." If you're using sound markers, you and the student can pull down the sound markers together for each sound, saying the sounds as the markers are moved into the squares.

Data Recording

When you are teaching phonemic awareness, pay close attention to your students' responses. When errors are made, note what kinds of errors they are making:

- Are they able to do complete phoneme segmentation?
- Are they able to auditorially blend the phoneme-separated words that you give them?
- Are they confusing sounds? Example: saying /b/ for /p/, or /t/ for /d/.
- Do they consistently miss the last sounds or middle sounds in words?

Use the following box as a sample recording form.

Phonemic Awareness

Provide words when discussing errors.

1. Student does this well: (circle)

   initial ending middle segmentation blending

2. Student errors: (circle)

   initial ending middle segmentation blending

3. Sound confusion?

A specific notation about a student's performance will be very valuable feedback to the student's teacher. You will be an important asset to the reading program when you provide feedback that will help determine instruction for students.

Practice It: Phonemic Awareness

Exercise #6:

Use the following story from the *Read Well* reading program (Sprick, Howard, & Fidanque, 1999). Find 10 one-syllable words to practice phonemic awareness instruction. Then form pairs and role-play student and tutor with each other. Practice phonemic-awareness instruction using word play and each of the multisensory cues. When you are in the student role, make a few intentional errors to give your partner practice with error handling and data recording.

Choose 10 single-syllable words from the story and write them here. Order your words from simple to complex. For example, words with two sounds will come before words with three sounds, and these will be followed by words with initial blends and words having final blends.

1. ____________________
2. ____________________
3. ____________________
4. ____________________
5. ____________________
6. ____________________
7. ____________________
8. ____________________
9. ____________________
10. ____________________

Funny Weather Facts

One summer day, in a small English town, clouds began to darken the sky. People expected an afternoon shower. However, when the rain started to fall it was more than just a shower. The people could hear funny sounds. Whack! Plop, plop, plop! Plop, plop, whack! Everyone ran indoors. Then they started to see funny things in the rain.

"What is happening?" the people asked.

A little kid said, "I think it's raining cats and dogs." Everyone laughed. A man said, "Maybe the sky is falling!" Another man asked, "Do you think it could be something from another planet?" Just then, someone else shouted, "Wow! That rain is hopping, and it's green!"

The people shouted all together, "It's raining frogs!"

Do you think this story is fact or fiction? It is an odd story, but it is a real story.

(continued) **Exercise #6**

Use two of the words to practice teaching the following phonemic awareness tasks. List a multi-sensory cue you will use to teach each of the following skills. For example, you might select *Tap the Sounds* to isolate initial sounds.

- Isolate Initial Sounds ______________________
- Isolate Final Sounds ______________________
- Isolate Middle Vowel Sounds ______________________
- Complete Segmentation ______________________
- Auditory Blending ______________________

Error Response:

1. Point out one thing that was done correctly.
2. Demonstrate the correct way.
3. Point out the place where a correction was made. Explain.
4. Student does it again with you, together.

Data Record:

Phonemic Awareness

Provide words when discussing errors.

1. Student does this well: (circle)

   initial ending middle segmentation blending

2. Student errors: (circle)

   initial ending middle segmentation blending

3. Sound confusion?

Review: Phonemic Awareness

1. On what reading skill is Chapter 1 based? ________________

2. Why is this a critical skill? ________________

3. Where will you find words to use for teaching phonemic awareness? How will you know which are the best words to choose and use for phoneme awareness lessons? ________________

4. Describe two procedures for teaching phonemic awareness. ________________

(continued) **Review:** Phonemic Awareness

5. What do you do if your student makes an error? ____________________

6. Be ready to demonstrate your ability to segment and blend phonemes with your trainer.

Chapter 2: Phonics

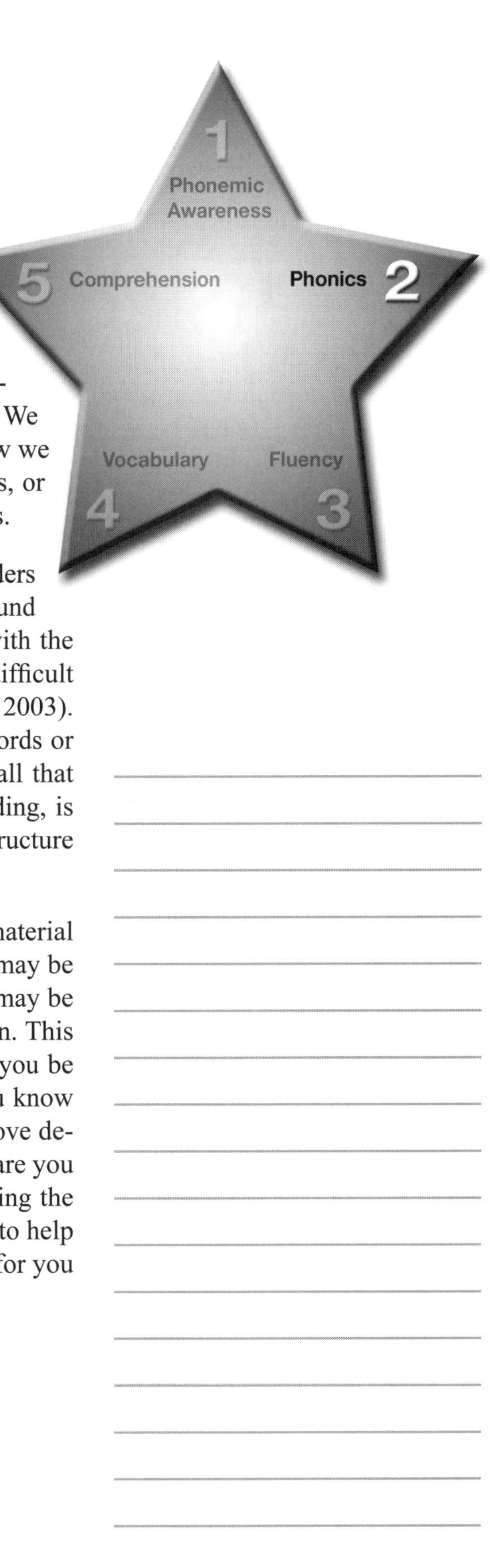

Discussion

A young or struggling reader faces tasks similar to those of a detective. Detectives decode mysteries, and readers decode words. Fortunately for readers, there is a consistent set of sounds that can be applied to letters and groups of letters to solve their mysteries. This application of sounds to letters to decode words is called *phonics*. We learned about *phonemic awareness* in the first chapter. Now we will take those same sounds and map them onto the letters, or *graphemes*, that are used to visually represent those sounds.

Studies have shown that the first strategy proficient readers apply when they come across an unfamiliar word is to sound it out. Studies that compare poor readers' brain activity with the brain activity of accomplished readers demonstrate how difficult this decoding process is for the struggling reader (Shaywitz, 2003). We also know that when students spend time analyzing words or decoding them, they are more likely to automatically recall that word the next time they come across it. Phonics, or decoding, is the application of analysis that originates from the basic structure of our written language.

Your school will most likely provide you with reading material that requires the teaching of phonics. The reading lessons may be direct and clearly outlined with a script to follow, or they may be vague, with little direction provided for phonics instruction. This wide possible range of instructional support requires that you be prepared and confident in your phonics skills and that you know how to apply basic instruction to help young readers improve decoding skills. Chapter 2 of *ParaReading* training will prepare you to use the instructional materials that are provided. Knowing the sounds of the letters and letter combinations and the ways to help students learn and recall those sounds are important skills for you to have.

Your Turn to Learn

A good place to start when preparing to teach phonics skills is with a review of the individual sound-symbol relationships most common in our written language. As a tutor, you must:

- Demonstrate proficiency with the most common sound-symbol relationships.
- Use a multisensory teaching approach when decoding words.
- Work with instructional materials to teach phonics.

Phonemes are the *sounds* of our language; graphemes are the *written letters or groups of letters* that represent the phonemes. Phonemes are the spoken elements, and graphemes are the written symbols for phonemes. When we teach *phonemic awareness*, we ask students to provide *sounds*; when we teach *phonics*, we ask students to match *letters* to the sounds. Each is an aspect of language. Phonemic awareness is spoken language, but phonics requires the visual recognition of letters and letter patterns.

Tutors Know! Phonemes are the sounds, and Phonics adds the letters! *Phonemes* = oral language. *Phonics* = oral language plus letters!

With phonics, we teach children to match letters to sounds:

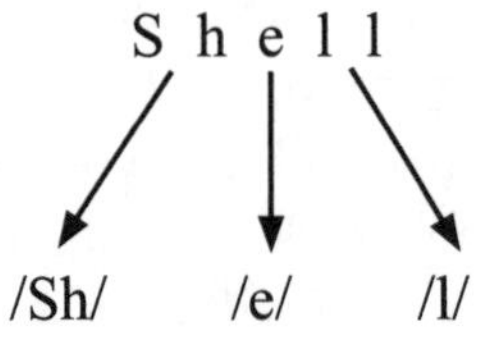

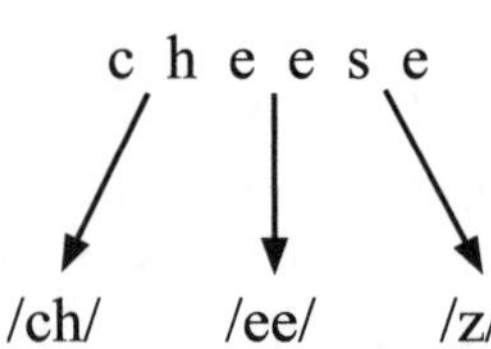

Exercise #7: Phonemic Awareness or Phonics: Which One Is It?

Follow your trainer's directions to create phonics and phonemic awareness response cards for this activity. Listen to the sample teaching prompts. Determine if the students are being asked to use phonemic awareness or phonics, and hold up either the ***Phonemic Awareness*** or the ***Phonics*** card to show which focus skill is called for.

1. How many sounds in *bat*?
2. Sound out this written word: *rug*.
3. What silent letter is at the end of *game*?
4. What letter makes the sound "/s/"?
5. "/f/ /r/ /o/ /g/" What word?
6. Spell the longest word you know.
7. Tell me the middle sound in *mom*.
8. Tap the sounds in *lake*.
9. Find another word that ends with an *-m*.
10. Say *bed* without "/b/."
11. What two letters say "/sh/."
12. Spell the first syllable in *cracker*.
13. Change the /ŏ/ in cop to /ă/. What's the word?

Review and Practice: Phonics

Exercise #8: Making Grapheme Tiles

Welcome to the Grid! Use Grid One (a reproducible copy is available at the end of the workbook) to record the graphemes with their associated sounds as your trainer presents them. Each sound is presented with a key word that will help you recall the correct pronunciation of the letter sound.

When you are finished, practice saying the sounds randomly with a partner. Take turns, point to the letters, and randomly ask your partner to say the sounds for the graphemes. Help each other. Your trainer will come around and check for accuracy.

Tutors Know! *Grapheme*: The letter or letters that are used to represent and spell one sound. *–igh* is a grapheme for /ie/, and *–ea* is a grapheme for /ee/.

Exercise #9: Making Pairs of Words

Cut out the letter tiles in Grid Two (a reproducible copy is available at the end of the workbook). Arrange the graphemes in front of you as directed by your trainer.

Single vowel spellings: o, u, i

Consonants: n, b, g, l, s, m, p

Digraphs: th, ng, sh

Vowel spellings: aw, oo, ur, ee

Create the following groups of letter tiles, and follow your trainer's directions to practice decoding using "minimal" pairs of words—words that differ by only one sound! Record the words you make for later reference. Have fun!

Set One: o, u, g, m, s, l, b

____

Set Two: oo, i, ur, aw, l, s, n, p

____

Set Three: o, i, ee, ng, th, s, l, n, sh

____

Grid One

Grid Two

o	u	i	a			
n	b	g	l	s	m	p
th	ng	sh				
aw	oo	ur	ee			
f	t					
r	c					

Nonsense Words

When we want to check a student's ability to sound out words, to decode, we give them nonsense words. These are "make-believe" words that give us a sense of how well students are able to figure out unfamiliar *real* words when they come across them in their reading. Listen and follow along while your trainer decodes the following nonsense words.

vog	tel	ut
zek	zub	pef
trum	blesh	splin
gake	pune	lete
tark	yort	mir
soik	zail	shay
quawp	woam	prew

Exercise #10

Take turns with your partner and decode these same words. You will be asked to read a *new* set of nonsense words to your trainer during the review.

How to Teach It: Phonics

Most remedial reading lessons teach phonics skills from the "bottom up." This means that the lesson begins with the phonic elements and builds to a syllable or word. For example, to teach the digraph *sh*, the sound /sh/ is introduced. The grapheme is presented, then single words with *sh* are provided for practice. The words are presented in sentences, then paragraphs. This provides students with teacher support during the initial stages of learning a new concept and the gradual ascent to independent reading. It also gives students ample opportunity to practice the new skill.

Example	Level
The dish was full of shiny shells. The shrimp did not shed their shells, so there were no shrimp shells to show them.	paragraph
The ship went to find big shells under the water.	sentence
ship, dish	words
sh written	grapheme
/sh/	sound

Tutors Know! Much of a paraeducator's teaching responsibility is to provide the important *review* and *practice* that students at risk desperately need to strengthen and build their reading skills. *Review* means that information introduced at an earlier time is revisited. *Practice* means that additional time is spent applying and using the new skills.

Teaching Individual Letter Sounds

Tutors Know! *Movable Letters* (*Letter Tiles*) are a tool that increases a child's interaction with the process of decoding and spelling. Movable letters may be actual letter shapes or letters printed on squares of paper.

Before the strategies for teaching decoding *words* are introduced, it is important to discuss the student who is at the very early stages of decoding and just learning the *sounds* for individual letters. This student will require drill and practice to begin connecting the sounds to letters before blending them into words. To assist with this process, the teacher presents the letters and provides the sounds that are associated with the letters. Moveable letters provide a great tool for teaching the early stages of decoding.

Exercise #11
Find the following graphemes that you cut from Grid Two:

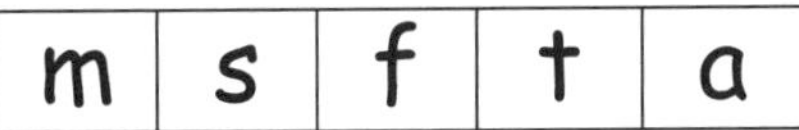

m	s	f	t	a

Role-play with your trainer. You will be the student, and your trainer will be the tutor. Follow the directions with your moveable letters to experience how to teach letter sounds.

Procedure for Teaching Letter Sounds:

1. "This letter *m* makes the sound /m/. Say it with me, /m/. What sound does the *m* (pointing) make?" "When we see *m* in a word, we say /m/."

   Follow the same process for each letter, teaching the sounds.

2. Point randomly to the letters, asking for the sounds. Point and say, "What sound?" Keep a quick pace. Make it lively: "I am going to try to trick you…"
3. Ask the student to show you a given sound. "Show me the /s/. Show me the /ă/."

Exercise #12
Pair up and role-play student and tutor. Use the following grapheme tiles:

p	n	r	c	o

Practice the previous steps for introducing and practicing the individual letter sounds.

Teach the letter sounds and then ask two types of questions to provide extra practice:

- "Show me the /_/ sound."
- Pointing to a letter: "What sound is this?"

Procedures For Teaching Blending

This section outlines four procedures that you can use to teach decoding and blending skills:

1. Whole-Word Blending
2. Stretch-and-Say Blending
3. Tap and Blend
4. Sounds to Spelling—This method uses the *encoding* or spelling process as a way of practicing and recalling the graphemes that are used to represent sounds.

Whole-Word Blending

Another name for this procedure is "touch and say." Children touch each letter (or grapheme), say the sounds, and then blend the sounds to read the word.

Step-by-step procedure for decoding *shack*:

1. Point to the digraph *sh* at the beginning of *shack*. Say "sound"; students say "/sh/."
2. Touch each successive grapheme, saying "sound" for each one, /sh/ /a/ /k/, as the children make the sound that each grapheme stands for. Then go back and blend the whole word smoothly, running your finger under the word, left to right, at the rate of about one phoneme each half second.

   Continuous sounds are easier to begin with. For example, *bat* (/b/ /a/ /t/) and *check* (/ch/ /e/ /ck/) are a little harder than *shell*, *thin*, or *moss*.
3. Slowly compress the extended word. Go from *shshshaaack* to *shshaack* to *shack*.
4. Point to the word and say, "The word is *shack*."
5. Check for understanding of the word and the ability to use it in a sentence.

Role-play Whole-Word Blending with your trainer.

Stretch-and-Say Blending

Phonemes are segmented and counted and then the whole word is blended with an accompanying gesture to pull the sounds together into the word.

Step-by-step procedure for decoding *sun*:

1. Say the whole word, "Sun."
2. Ask students to hold up one finger for each sound they hear as the word is segmented and the phonemes counted.
3. Say the whole word while pulling your arm down or sweeping it across your body from left to right.

Role-play Stretch-and-Say Blending with your trainer.

Tap and Blend

This method is similar to Whole-Word Blending except that the student is actively involved with the decoding process through *tapping* the sounds as tutor and student work through the word together.

Step-by-step procedure for decoding *stick*:

In unison, tutor and student tap index finger and thumb together as they say each sound in the word and blend the sounds together. If needed, the tutor can touch each grapheme as the student taps the sounds.

1. Tap and say "/s/."
2. Tap and say "/t/."
3. Tap and say "/ĭ/."
4. Tap and say "/k/."
5. Run finger under whole word and say, "Stick."

Tap and Blend adds a multisensory element that assists the student with connecting the individual sounds with the letters in words. As with any decoding method, children progress from oral decoding of words to silent decoding. Some students need more time to decode orally before transitioning to silent decoding and then to automatic decoding of unfamiliar words.

Role-play Tap and Blend with your trainer.

Sounds to Spelling—Phoneme Grapheme Mapping

This method adds another very closely related skill to the decoding process: encoding. The student separates the sounds in a word and applies the grapheme for those sounds. That is, the student *spells* the word.

You will need the following materials:

- Copies of the Sounds to Spelling form or a sheet of paper with boxes and lines.
- Moveable sound markers—paper squares or little crackers, some small items that the students can use to represent the separate phonemes.
- Carefully chosen words from the student's reading materials.

Step-by-step procedure for decoding *book*:

1. Tutor says, "Book."
2. Student repeats the word and moves markers into boxes for each separate sound, saying the sounds as the markers are touched and moved—"/b/ /ŏŏ/ /k/."
3. The tutor asks two types of questions about the sounds: "Show me the /k/," and then, pointing to the second sound marker, "What is this sound?" Student says, "/ŏŏ/." These two questions can be repeated for different sounds in the word so that the student is responding to questions about all of the represented sounds.
4. Once the questions have been asked, the student is instructed to push up the markers one at a time and write the graphemes for each sound in the spaces, saying the sounds as the letters are written.
5. The student then writes the entire word on the line.

Role-play Sounds to Spelling with your trainer. Use the Sounds to Spelling form; a reproducible copy is available at the end of the workbook.

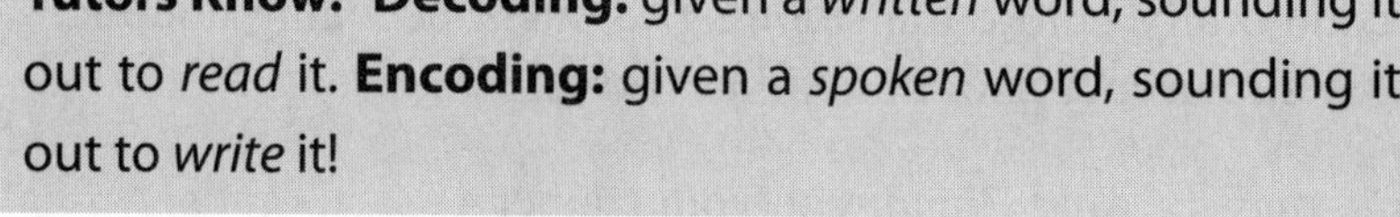
Tutors Know! Decoding: given a *written* word, sounding it out to *read* it. **Encoding:** given a *spoken* word, sounding it out to *write* it!

Sounds to Spelling

Student: ______________________ Date: ______________

____

____

____

Practice It: Phonics

The use of moveable letters to teach letter-sound correspondence and four instructional strategies for decoding whole words were introduced in the previous section. Now it is time for you to practice using these strategies to begin building confidence and automaticity with their use. Additional practice with children is recommended. The following role-playing activities are designed to provide experience with each of the four strategies. Practice the Error Response procedure when the "student" makes errors. Record data as instructed on the data form provided.

Error Response

1. Point out one part that was done correctly. "This first sound is /s/; you were right!"
2. Demonstrate the correct way. "Watch and listen while I do it." Decode each sound correctly, and blend the sounds to say the word.
3. Point out the place where a correction was made. "This middle sound here (pointing) is /ŏ/; I heard you say /ŭ/. What sound will you say next time?"
4. Student does it again with you. "Do it correctly with me."

Exercise #13: Individual Letter Sounds

Pair up and take turns as student and tutor to role-play the steps for introducing and practicing individual letter sounds. When you role-play the student, make a few errors to give your partner practice with the error-response process.

- Tutor #1 uses the following letter squares: p, n, r, c, o.
- Tutor #2 uses the following letter squares: d, h, k, l, i.

Directions:

1. "This letter *m* makes the sound /m/. Say it with me, /m/. What sound does the *m* (pointing) make?" " When we see *m* in a word, we say /m/."

   Follow the same process for each letter, teaching the sounds.

2. Point randomly to the letters, asking for the sounds. Point and say, "What sound?" Keep a quick pace. Make it lively: "I am going to try to trick you…."
3. Ask the student to show you a given sound. "Show me the /s/. Show me the /ă/."

Data Recording

Provide recording data during your role-playing practice.

1. Student does this well:

2. Student errors:

3. Sound confusion?

Exercise #14: Whole-Word Blending

Pair up and practice the steps for Whole-Word Blending. When you role-play the student, make a few errors to give your partner practice with the error-response process.

Please note that /ar/, /ou/, and /ee/ stand for single vowel sounds.

- Tutor #1 uses the following words: *crash, swim, steep.*
- Tutor #2 uses the following words: *brush, star, trout.*

Example—Whole-Word Blending

Step-by-step procedure for decoding *shack*:

1. Point to the digraph *sh* and say "Sound"; students say "/sh/."
2. Point to the *a* and say "Sound"; students say "/ă/."
3. Point to the *ck* and say "Sound"; students say "/k/."
4. Slide fingers under the whole word to blend it; students say "Shack."
5. Point to the word and say, "The word is *shack*."
6. Check for understanding and the ability to use the word in a sentence.

Data Recording

Provide words when discussing errors.

1. Student does this well:

2. Student errors:

3. Sound confusion?

Exercise #15: Stretch-and-Say Blending

Pair up and role-play the steps for introducing and practicing Stretch-and-Say Blending. When you role-play the student, make a few errors to give your partner practice with the error-response process.

- Tutor #1 uses the following words: *pine, tape, glue.*
- Tutor #2 uses the following words: *game, home, bike.*

Example—Stretch-and-Say Blending

Step-by-step procedure for decoding *sun*:

1 Say the whole word, "Sun."

2 Ask students to hold up one finger for each sound they hear as the word is segmented and the phonemes counted.

3 Say the whole word while pulling your arm down or sweeping it across your body from left to right.

Data Recording

Provide words when discussing errors.

1. Student does this well:

2. Student errors:

3. Sound confusion?

Exercise #16: Tap and Blend

Pair up and role-play the steps for introducing and practicing Tap and Blend. When you role-play the student, make a few errors to give your partner practice with the error-response process.

- Tutor #1 uses the following words: *lunch*, *harsh*, *turn*.
- Tutor #2 uses the following words: *tooth*, *clay*, *boots*.

Example—Tap and Blend

Step-by-step procedure for decoding *stick*:

In unison, the teacher and student tap index finger and thumb together as they say each sound in the word and blend the sounds together. If needed, the teacher can touch each grapheme as the student taps the sounds.

1. Tap and say "/s/."
2. Tap and say "/t/."
3. Tap and say "/ĭ/."
4. Tap and say "/k/."
5. Run finger under whole word and say, "Stick."

Data Recording

Provide words when discussing errors.

1. Student does this well:
2. Student errors:
3. Sound confusion?

Exercise #17: Sounds to Spelling

Pair up and role-play the steps for practicing Sounds to Spelling using the Sounds to Spelling form. When you role-play the student, make a few errors to give your partner practice with the error-response process.

- Tutor #1 uses the following words: *bricks, farming, paint.*
- Tutor #2 uses the following words: *white, thirsty, healing.*

Example—Sounds to Spelling

Step-by-step procedure for decoding *book*:

1. Tutor says, "Book."
2. Student repeats the word and moves markers into the spaces for each separate sound, saying the sounds as the markers are touched and moved—"/b/ /ŏŏ/ /k/."
3. The tutor asks two types of questions about the sounds: "Show me the /k/," and then, pointing to the second sound marker, "What is this sound?" Student says, "/ŏŏ/." These two questions can be repeated for different sounds in the word so that the student is responding to questions about all of the represented sounds.
4. Once the questions have been asked, the student is instructed to push up the markers one at a time and write the graphemes for each sound in the spaces, saying the sounds as the letters are written.
5. The student then writes the entire word on the line.

Data Recording

Provide words when discussing errors.

1. Student does this well:

2. Student errors:

3. Sound confusion?

Review: Phonics

1. What skill is practiced in Chapter 2? ______

2. Name and describe two blending processes used to teach decoding in Chapter 2. ______

3. What is the benefit of recording a student's performance when decoding? ______

4. Describe the steps for responding to student errors. ______

5. Be ready to decode a selection of nonsense words for the trainer.

Chapter 3: Fluency

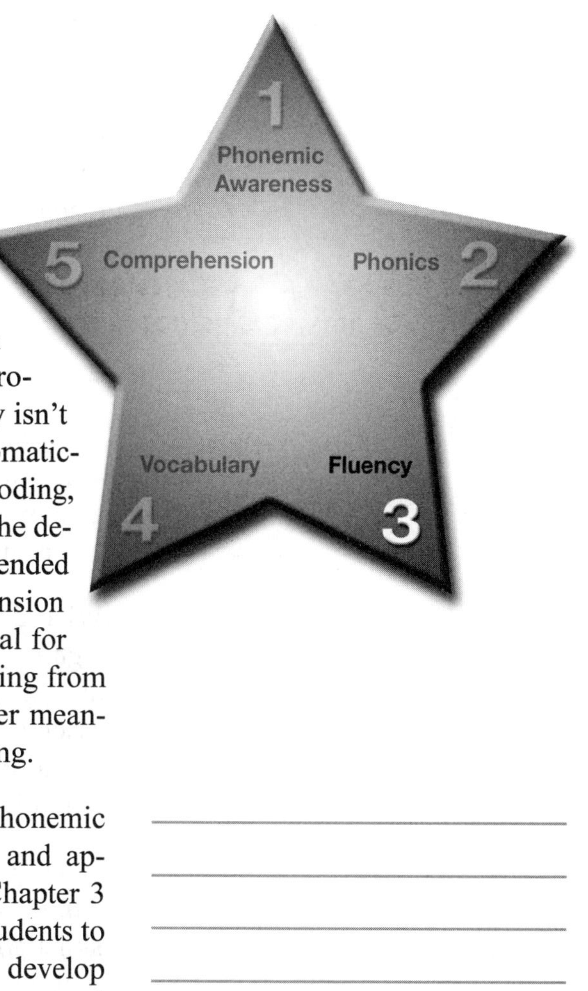

Discussion

The ultimate goal of reading instruction is for students to be automatic with the skills they use to read. Just like learning to play a musical instrument or ride a bicycle, there are underlying reading skills that, with practice and time, reach a level of ease that allows the process to happen effortlessly. Reaching this level of fluency isn't always easy. When students read fluently, they have automaticity with other reading skills: phonemic awareness, decoding, and word recognition. When a student is a fluent reader, the demanding tasks of decoding are automatic, and energy expended during the reading process can be directed to comprehension of the material that is being read. This is the ultimate goal for our students: to become fluent readers able to gain meaning from the written word, apply higher-order thinking skills, infer meaning, and expand their knowledge of the world from reading.

The first two chapters in *ParaReading* taught us about phonemic awareness through sound segmentation and blending, and applying letters to sounds through phonics and spelling. Chapter 3 builds on this instruction and focuses on working with students to build *automaticity* with these skills so that students can develop fluent reading habits. Previous studies have shown that trained tutors play an important role with helping young readers to significantly improve reading fluency (Glaser, 2002).

What does it mean to read fluently? What does a person sound like when they read fluently? What can fluent readers do that non-fluent readers are unable to do? These questions will be answered in this chapter.

Your Turn to Learn

Listen to your trainer simulate two different students reading. Answer these questions:

- What does a fluent reader sound like?
- What does a disfluent reader sound like?
- What do you think are the advantages of being able to read fluently?

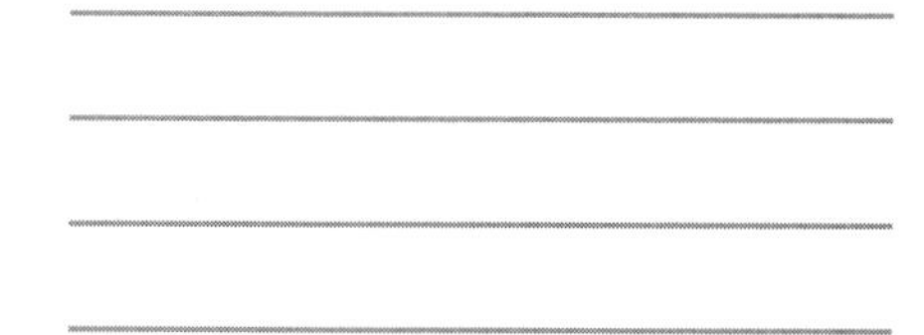

How do students become fluent readers? Many become fluent readers from lots of practice with reading, similar to the practice that is commonly prescribed to improve musical or athletic performance. Repeated skill practice improves the performance of a skill. To improve reading fluency for many students at risk, it takes reading practice plus additional *fluency training*. Fluency training is the instructional focus of Chapter 3. But first, let's look at the processes involved in the task of reading fluently.

Eye-Voice Span

Eye-voice span enables us to move our eyes ahead of our voice when we read. Your trainer will lead you through an activity that will provide you with an opportunity to experience eye-voice span.

What do you notice when the projected image is removed from sight? The trainer is able to continue reading a few words even after the image disappears! This ability is characteristic of fluent readers. When the reading process is automatic, our conscious attention is focused on meaning, and our eyes move ahead of our voice.

Helping students become fluent readers begins with teaching phonemic awareness and decoding skills. A firm grounding with these skills allows them to read isolated words and build automaticity with sight recognition. The frequent reading of connected text, sentences, and stories helps young students become fluent. Many students require special attention to reach levels of fluency that will allow them to progress with their reading skills. The common instructional process is to have the student read material several times until they attain fluency with the material. This practice is called *repeated readings*.

Repeated readings provide fluency training with:

- Letter decoding
- Single-word decoding
- Reading connected text

Repeated Readings

Fluency has been a focus of key reading research over the past several years. Reading fluency is measured by words read correctly per minute (WCPM) during the reading of instructional level material over three consecutive readings of the same material. The following activity has been prepared to provide an opportunity for you to experience the process and effects of repeated readings.

Exercise #18: Building Fluency with the Unfamiliar

Your trainer will take you through an exercise designed to help you experience improved fluency through the use of repeated readings. It is impossible for an adult to entirely duplicate the experience of a young child, but this practice comes close. During the process, pay attention to your responses, observations, and any questions that arise. Jot them down for discussion.

1. What were your initial reactions to the text? ______

2. What are your observations with each successive reading? ______

3. Did your initial responses to the text change with exposure through repeated readings? How? ______

How to Teach It: Fluency

The steps for using **repeated readings** are outlined below and can be used with students from a variety of reading levels. Repeated readings can be used to build fluency with individual letter sounds, isolated words, and with reading passages.

Tutors Know! *Isolated words* means that words are presented alone, separate from connected or story text. A word list provides isolated words.

- If your students are just beginning to learn **letter sounds**, repeated readings are to be done with a page of letters from which letter sounds will be read.
- If your students are **decoding and blending single words** to practice building automaticity, do repeated readings with isolated words that reflect the target decoding skills.
- Once your students are reading **passages of text such as paragraphs and stories**, use these texts for repeated readings. This level of repeated reading generally begins around mid-first grade.

Materials You Will Need to Do the Repeated Readings:

- ***Reading material that is written at an instructional level for your student.*** This can be had in many ways: 1) Ask the classroom teacher to recommend appropriate reading material; 2) Use the classroom reading curriculum; 3) Use reading fluency training passages that are grade leveled and provide counted words for you.
- ***A copy of the page the student will be reading.*** You will use this to record student errors.
- ***A stopwatch.*** This is a necessary tool.
- ***Three colored markers or colored pencils to record the errors.*** Use one color for each reading to visually separate the errors in the first, second, and third readings.
- ***A copy of the Fluency Training: Repeated Readings Chart.*** A reproducible version is available at the end of the workbook.

Repeated Readings

Step-by-Step Process

Instruct the student: "Please read this passage for your fluency training today. Begin reading here (point), and read until I tell you to stop. If you come to a word you don't know, I will tell you the word." Time him for one minute, and note the number of words he reads. Subtract the errors for a total of words correct per minute (WCPM).

1. Chart the WCPM on the Fluency Training: Repeated Readings Chart. Show the student how to graph his own performance.

2. Review the errors with the student. Show and tell him the words you helped him with, words he omitted or substituted, and words he hesitated with.

3. Instruct the student to read the passage again, and follow the same procedure.

4. Do this for a total of three times, marking the errors with a different color each time. Have the student graph his performance after each reading. Work with the student to set goals between readings—"How many words can you read next time? Can you beat your time?"

Tutors Know! *WCPM* means "words read correctly per minute." The total number of words that a student correctly reads in one minute is that student's WCPM.

Reading Errors

When you do repeated readings, you will also need to know what to count as a reading error. The following guidelines tell you what to count as a reading error:

- *Unknown word.* The student hesitates or attempts to read a word but does not produce the correct word in three seconds. Provide the correct word for the student and mark it as an error on your sheet.

- *Substitution.* The student misreads a word, substituting a different word for the actual word in the text.

- *Omission.* The student leaves a word out while reading.

Fluency Training: Repeated Readings Chart

Student Name: ____

Date: ______________ Reading Selection: ______________ ______________	Date: ______________ Reading Selection: ______________ ______________	Date: ______________ Reading Selection: ______________ ______________

Words Read Correctly Per Minute											
	120										120
	100										100
	90										90
	80										80
	70										70
	60										60
	50										50
	40										40
	30										30
	20										20
	10										10
	0										0
		1	2	3	1	2	3	1	2	3	

Do not count as errors:

- Rereading words or phrases
- Self-corrections made within three seconds
- Skipping a line (Do not count the words in the omitted line as errors.)

Exercise #19

There are several steps to follow when using repeated readings to improve reading fluency. Your trainer will now take you through each of the repeated readings steps with sample text. Review what to count as *reading errors* with a partner prior to going through the process, and then practice the process. Use the text and repeated readings chart provided.

Listen to your trainer read this passage three times. Follow along during the three separate readings, and note errors. Record the WCPM after each reading. Be ready to discuss your experiences.

(continued) **Exercise #19**

All About Plants

There are many plants on our earth. Plants can be big. Plants can be 14
small. We can't even see some plants. They are too small. Plants need many 28
things to grow. They need sunlight. Some plants need a lot of sunlight. 41
Others need very little sunlight. Plants need water to grow. Just like 54
sunlight, some plants need a lot of water. Other plants need very little 67
water. A cactus can live without a lot of water. 77

Plants also need food from the soil to grow. Plants use their roots to 91
get food and water from the soil. The roots also hold up the plant. The 106
leaves make food for the plant. They use the sun to make food. Stems are 121
different on plants. The stems hold up the leaves and flowers on the plant. It 136
also carries water and food to the plant. The stem of a tree is hard and 152
strong. The stem of a flower can bend easily. Plants have seeds to grow new 167
plants. Some seeds are very small. Other seeds are in fruit that grows on the 182
plants. Some plants have flowers. Other plants do not have flowers. Plants 194
give us many things. They are good to us. 203

Words Read Correctly Per Minute				
100				
90				
80				
70				
60				
50				
40				
30				
20				
10				
0				
	1	2	3	

Practice It: Fluency

Exercise #20

Form small groups of three or four. Use the sample repeated readings practice pages to practice repeated readings. There is one example for each of the three levels of beginning reader: letter sounds, isolated words, and connected text.

- Listen to the trainer simulate a child's timed performance.
- Record errors on the text as you listen.
- Record WCPM on the chart at the close of each minute's reading.
- Discuss, compare errors, analysis, and data recording with the other members of your group before the next reading.

(continued) **Exercise #20**

Repeated Readings Sample 1: Letter Sounds

Say the letter sounds.

i	th	g	l	s	b	h	g	w	sh	a	u	12
h	f	x	e	a	ch	p	n	t	o	v	m	24
p	qu	s	y	n	c	d	j	r	sh	d	y	36
b	e	th	z	m	k	l	x	a	n	i	p	48
r	ch	s	y	t	th	qu	f	v	g	d	e	60

Number of Sounds Read Correctly

100
90
80
70
60
50
40
30
20
10
0

1 2 3

(continued) **Exercise #20**

Repeated Readings Sample 2: Isolated Words

fed	cut	fed	kid	then	pan	6
net	path	wet	fad	rut	lop	12
then	wet	kip	dub	that	fat	18
rug	that	bag	peg	rug	let	24
pen	bath	than	fed	did	log	30
thin	dad	fad	thin	bath	fell	36
bib	this	peg	path	pen	that	42
rut	kid	keg	net	get	pill	48
did	that	jam	bib	dad	dug	54
get	gum	kit	wet	cut	lid	60

Number of Sounds Read Correctly

100
90
80
70
60
50
40
30
20
10
0

1 2 3

(continued) **Exercise #20**

A History of Flight: Hot Air Balloons

For thousands of years, people dreamed of traveling in the air like birds. The only 15
problem was, people had no way to fly. Then, about two hundred years ago, two French 31
brothers made a big balloon. They lit a small fire under the balloon and watched as the 49
balloon rose in the air. Their balloon was flying! 57

Would you like to understand how the hot air balloon could fly? Hot air is lighter 73
than cold air. When the brothers lit the fire, as the air got hotter, it got lighter, and the 92
balloon began to fly. What do you think happened when the air in the balloon got cold? 109

The brothers put a rooster, a sheep, and a duck on the first flight of their balloon. 126
Before long, many people rode in hot air balloons. 135

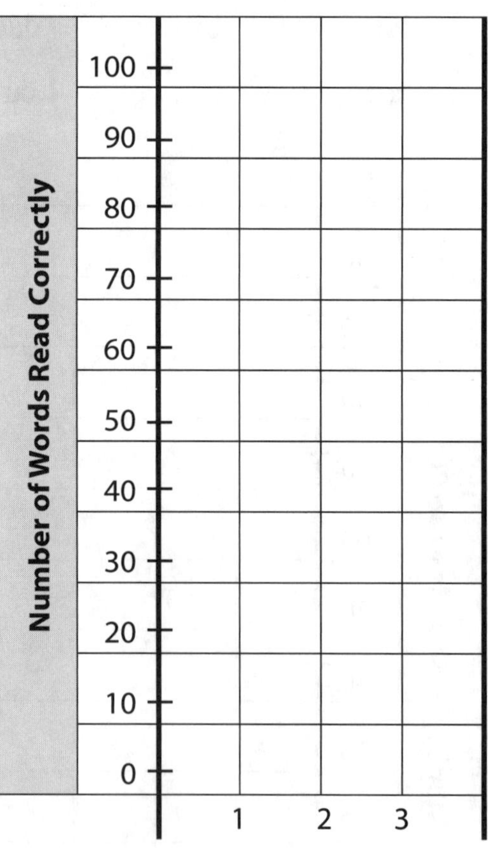

Review: Fluency

1. Why is reading fluency a critical skill for students to improve? ______________________________

2. What process do effective tutors use to help students improve reading fluency? Explain.

3. What will you count as errors during repeated readings? ______________________________

4. What does not constitute an error? ______________________________

5. List, in order, the first three skills that have been introduced in *ParaReading* and an example of how to teach each skill. ______________________________

Chapter 4: Vocabulary

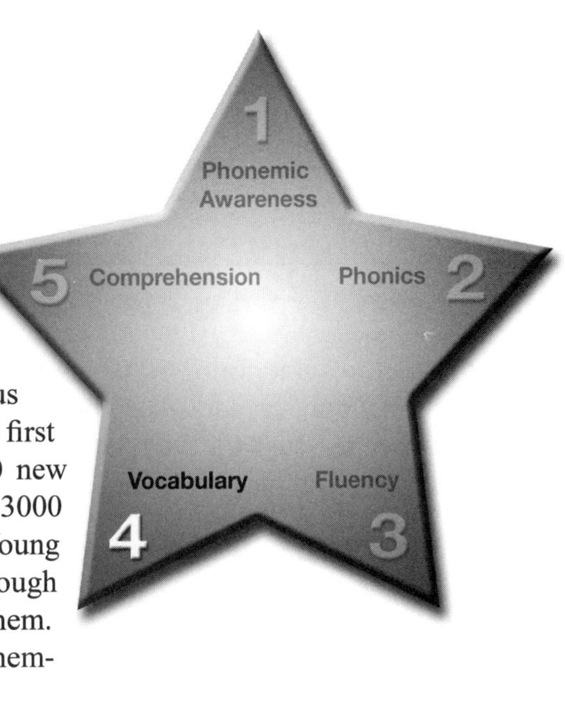

Discussion

What does it mean to *know* a word? How do people learn the *meanings* of words? Why is *vocabulary* an important reading skill? These questions have been asked and studied by reading researchers for many years. We have learned that knowing a word's meaning helps us recognize the word when we see it in print. We know that first and second grade children need to learn more than 800 new words per year and older children need to learn 2000 to 3000 new words a year to be considered effective readers. Young children learn a substantial number of these words through hearing when stories and informational text are read to them. Older children learn most new words through reading themselves (Biemiller, 1999; Nagy & Anderson, 1984).

Even though young children can and should learn word meanings through listening to text (both narrative stories and expository or informational texts), listening can only supplement and not replace critical reading practice for older children. These children need exposure to vocabulary through reading in order to build a visual reference of words for future reading fluency.

Yet, the reality is that many children come to school from environments where they receive limited exposure to language and therefore have fewer opportunities to build the vocabulary that would improve their reading comprehension. These kids are behind from the start, and it is critical that schools provide many opportunities for them to increase their vocabulary knowledge.

Phonemic awareness and phonics instruction prepare children to figure out new words when they are reading. Once those words are decoded, comprehension of the text is strengthened if the child *knows the meanings of the words*. There are four major processors that work together to help us read and comprehend what we read, as shown on the diagram on the next page. This model also provides us with a basis from which to evaluate and plan instruction for students. The *orthographic processor* is the first to receive input from the printed page. This visual information is combined with a word's phonological information to decode words. Once a word is decoded, the *meaning processor* matches it with a known word, and its meaning is accessed. If the word is unknown, then comprehension is jeopardized. It is important to know that once a word's meaning is stored in the word-meaning area of the brain, it is more easily recognized in print (Adams, 1990). Increasing a student's vocabulary not only helps to develop word *recognition*, it also improves *comprehension*. All of the processors work together during the process of reading.

Exercise #21: Experience the Processors At Work

Use the pictures and four-part processor model to learn more about how the brain processes information when we read. Place the pictures in the appropriate area to demonstrate which processor carries the load for the function given as your trainer takes you through a simulation of a child's reading and misplaced meaning!

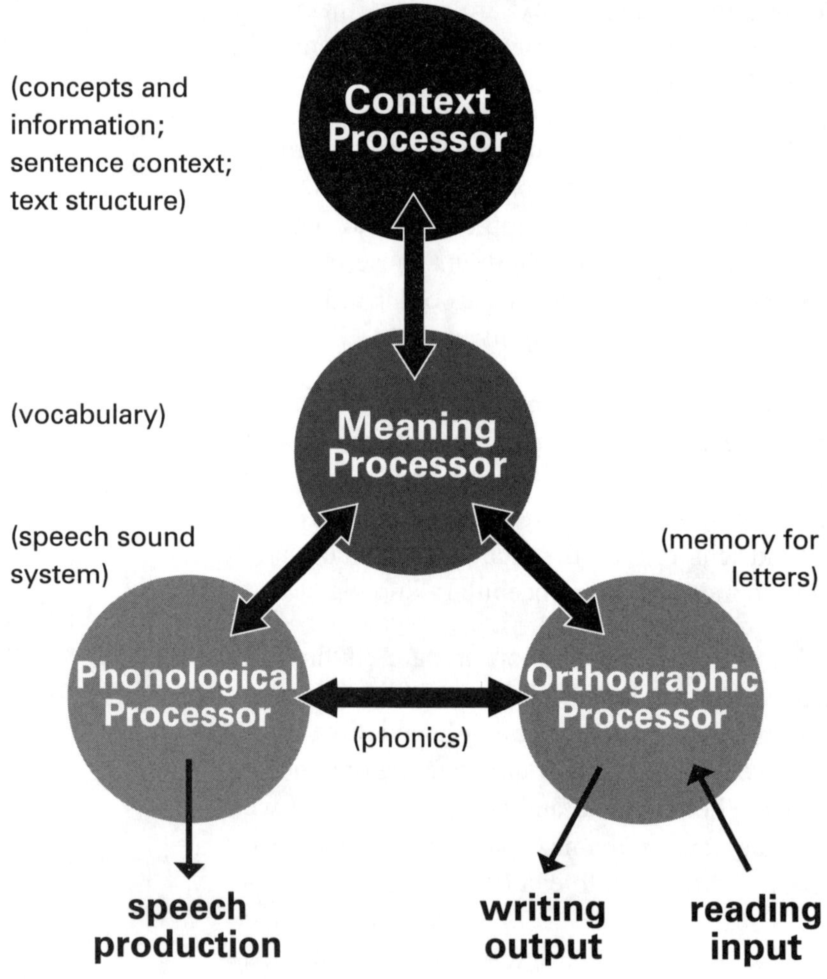

Your Turn to Learn

In this next section, you will participate in several exercises designed to increase your awareness of vocabulary and to prepare you to pay attention to vocabulary in your work with children. Are you ready? Here we go!

Context, Morphemes, and Figurative Language

The English language is called a complex or "deep" language because it has several origins, which affect spelling and pronunciation and help us determine meanings of words. As a result of its hybrid nature, English is a rich language.

To determine the meanings of words, we use several approaches:

- We consider the *context* in which the word is used. For example, the word *bug* has an obvious meaning that comes to mind: a little insect. However, when presented in the following context the meaning changes: "Her little brother would *bug* her by sneaking up on her and pulling her braid." Or, " The detective placed a *bug* in the car so he could listen to the conversation while they were driving."
- We consider the meaningful word parts, or *morphemes*. For example, the meaning of the word "semicircle" can be determined when we know that semi means part or one-half.
- We combine information from our personal experience and context to interpret *figurative language*. For example, in the sentence, "Her *heart sank* when she saw that the lottery numbers did not match her selection," the person's heart does not really drop. The expression means that she was disappointed and saddened.

Context—Read the following passage. What do you think the underlined word means? What information in the context helps you figure it out?

> It was fortunate that the vendor had a box of <u>buckshee</u> for the children to choose from, because they did not have a single penny to spend. (Bryson, 1990, p. 237)

Morphemes—With a partner, brainstorm as many words as you can think of that have the word part *struc(t)*. Example: instruction.

Share your collection of words with your trainer.

Given the collection of words, can you guess the meaning of the morpheme *struc*? Discuss.

Figurative Language—Beautiful and interesting verbal expression is created through figurative language. It is a common tool used by authors to enrich content and individualize their writing. Adults may intuit the meaning of figurative language more easily than children. For this reason, it is important that teachers be aware of the use of figurative language in the text that children will be listening to or reading and prepare them for it. This is especially true with English-language learners.

Find the figurative language in each of the following examples. Work with your group to come up with explanations that you would provide for your students. Tip: Tie the figurative language to your own experience and help the children connect with a personal experience of their own.

> My stomach flipped when I saw the cyclist approach the weakened wooden ramp at top speed.

> It was a crisp autumn morning, and the sunlight transformed the reds, yellows, and oranges into a hillside sunrise.

How to Teach It: Vocabulary

As a paraeducator, you can help motivate students to learn new words. The approaches described below provide simple ways to help children build interest in words and increase their understanding and use of vocabulary. Enjoy being the student as your trainer models each of the *ParaReading* vocabulary teaching components.

Choice Vocabulary—Wonder Words

Wonder Words are words or phrases (figurative language) that you anticipate may present comprehension difficulty for your students. Prepare students by *preteaching* the Wonder Words to improve the students' text comprehension.

There are two components to *ParaReading* vocabulary instruction:

- You, the tutor, choose the Wonder Words and provide definitions.
- Students use a Wonder Words journal to log the words.

Vocabulary instruction begins with finding Wonder Words in material that you will be reading to the students or that they will be reading themselves. Follow these steps:

- Preread the material that your students will be reading or that you will read to your students.
- Choose two words that meet the Wonder Words criteria: a) words or phrases that may be difficult to understand and that the students may hear or read again and therefore need to know; or b) words that may have multiple meanings.
- Provide information about the words' definitions.
- Use each word or phrase in a sentence related to the reading selection.
- Have the students tell you a sentence using each word and enter the words into their Wonder Words vocabulary journals.
- Review the Wonder Words the next time you meet with your students.

Exercise #22

Now it's your turn to experience the *ParaReading* vocabulary lesson. Your trainer will take you through each of the steps in the lesson. Follow directions as each of the steps is demonstrated. Take notes to help you remember the lesson content.

1. Material is previewed and two words or phrases are chosen.

____

____

2. Provide information about the words' definitions.

____

____

3. Use the words in sentences related to the reading selection.

____

____

4. Have the students tell you a sentence using the word and enter the word into their Wonder Words journal.

____

____

Wonder Words Journal Page

____

Vocabulary expansion occurs rapidly from birth through adolescence within communicative relationships. Everyday experiences with friends, caregivers, and community members shape speech habits and knowledge of language. The human mind latches onto new words as it hears them because they are the tools of communication. Humans have an intrinsic need to understand what is said to them and to share experience through language, and the brain is biologically adapted to support language acquisition. Before school and before learning to read, children learn most of the words they know through daily oral communication with adults. Adults facilitate that process when they introduce new words in a shared experience, elaborate what a child has said, confirm and clarify the child's attempts to use new words, deliberately repeat new words in conversation, or read aloud.

Practice It: Vocabulary

Your turn to try it! Pair up with a partner; one of you will be Tutor #1, and the other will be Tutor #2. Read through your corresponding reading selection, and follow steps 1–4 to prepare for a vocabulary lesson.

Tutor #1

Beware of Bears

Bears! Many people are fascinated by them. After all, who can resist a stuffed, cuddly teddy bear? Bear enclosures at zoos are often a popular exhibit. Watching adorable bear cubs romp brings smiles and chuckles from onlookers.

1. Preread the material.

2. Choose two **Wonder Words** that may present difficulty in understanding:

   ______________________ ______________________

3. Provide information about the words' definitions:

4. Provide examples of the words' usages in context:

Data Recording—Record student performance and the Wonder Words you chose using the following form.

Vocabulary—(circle one) **Listening or Reading**
Can the student use the vocabulary words in a sentence that shows he/she knows the word? Yes No
What were the Wonder Words?

Tutor #2

Camels: One Hump or Two?

Camels are funny-looking animals with humps on their backs. Camels are large animals. They are seven or eight feet tall. They have small heads but long, curved necks. Their legs are long, but their bodies are heavy. Camels are used for riding or for carrying heavy loads.

1. Preread the material.

2. Choose two Wonder Words that may present difficulty in understanding:

3. Provide information about the words' definitions:

4. Provide examples of the words' usages in context:

Data Recording—Record student performance and the Wonder Words you chose using the following form.

Vocabulary—(circle one) **Listening or Reading**
Can the student use the vocabulary words in a sentence that shows he/she knows the word? Yes No
What were the Wonder Words?

Now, #1 tutors get together, and #2 tutors get together. Compare your vocabulary choices and preparation. What are the similarities and differences? Why did you choose the words you did? Share your lesson preparations. What can we learn from each other?

OK, get back together with your partner. One of you will act as the tutor and the other as the student. Use the following guidelines to practice *ParaReading* vocabulary instruction. The tutor first writes the chosen words on the Wonder Word journal page (a reproducible version is available at the end of the workbook), and then the "student" writes sentences using the words or draws pictures of the words. Switch roles when you have successfully completed your role-play.

1. Show the written Wonder Words to the student (journal page). Read the words. “These are Wonder Words that you will be reading today.”
2. Read each word and provide definitions.
3. Tell about the word using the context of the story.
4. Have the student record a picture or brief definition in the Wonder Word journal to help recall the meaning.
5. Instruct the student to read the passage.
6. Record student performance using the data form.

Tip: Revisit the Wonder Words journal and discuss the words in relation to the story. Always encourage students to use the Wonder Words in their discussion. "Tell me about it, and use the word __________." Rephrase for the students if they do not use the Wonder Words. Provide opportunities for the students to apply the vocabulary to their own experiences.

Share role-play experiences with the whole group.

Wonder Words

Wonder Words

Review: Vocabulary

1. Describe the four-part processing system. Identify the four parts and tell how they work together to help gain meaning from written text.

2. Describe the process for choosing and defining the Wonder Words that you will teach your students.

3. Define *context*, and give an example of how it relates to teaching vocabulary.

4. Define *figurative language*, and tell how it relates to teaching vocabulary.

5. Define *morpheme*, and tell how morphemes relate to teaching and learning vocabulary.

6. What can you do to help your students remember the vocabulary you teach them?

Chapter 5: Comprehension

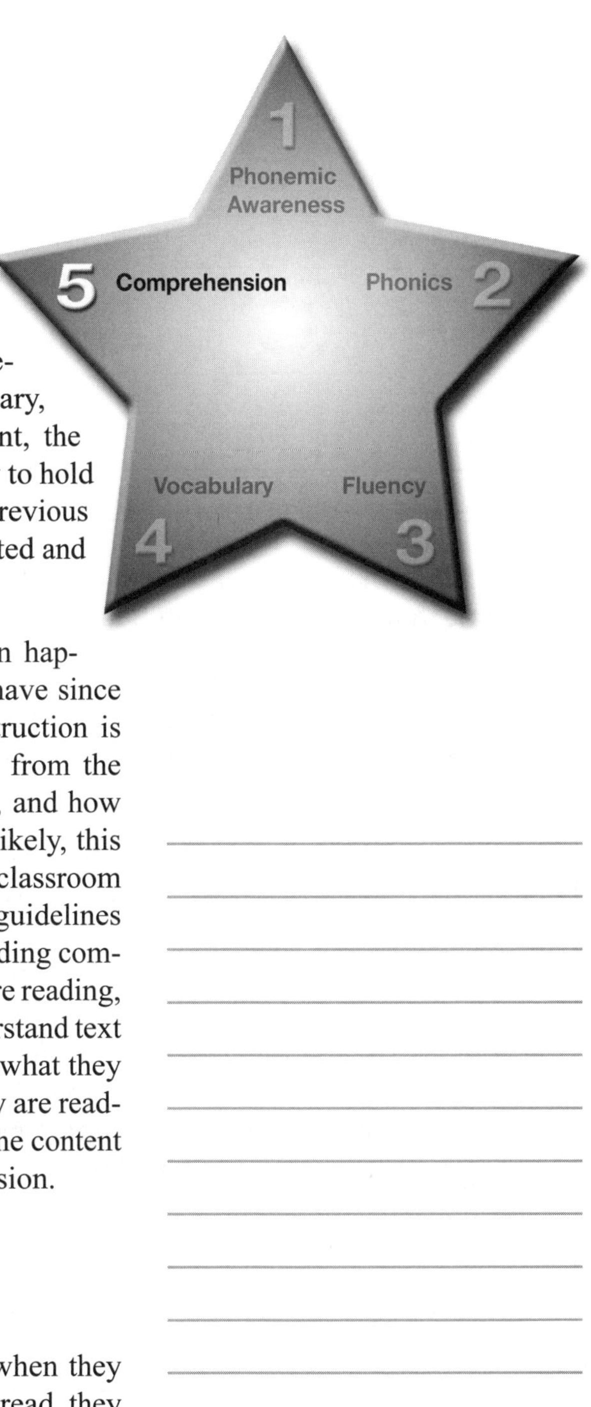

Discussion

Comprehension can be a complex process to identify and define. What does it mean to *you*? Comprehension has to do with *meaning*—deriving meaning from what we hear and what we read. Our ability to comprehend text depends on our understanding of the vocabulary, our previous experience and knowledge of the content, the simplicity or complexity of the text structure, our ability to hold onto the presented information and connect it with previous learning, and our language skills. This sounds complicated and it is! Teaching comprehension is not easy!

For many years, educators thought that comprehension happened as a natural outcome of the ability to read. We have since learned that this is not the case. Specific strategy instruction is required to teach the reader how to gain information from the text he reads, how to expand learning beyond the text, and how to combine meaning from several sources. More than likely, this intensive strategy instruction will take place within the classroom with whole-group instruction. *ParaReading* provides guidelines to help the paraeducator *support* the development of reading comprehension skills. Simple prompting or questioning before reading, during reading, and after reading can help students understand text as they read. Additionally, asking students to tell about what they have just read sends a message to students that what they are reading is important. Attending to the content and recalling the content of what they read plays an important role in comprehension.

Your Turn to Learn

You can help children improve comprehension skills when they read material or when you read to them. When children read, they exercise *reading comprehension*. When you read to children, they use *listening comprehension*. Whichever avenue a child uses to access the written material, we can use the same approach to support the development of comprehension skills. If your students have low reading skills, you may spend a portion of your time reading to them. You can use this opportunity to apply comprehension prompts. A prompt is a question or inquiry that initiates the comprehension process.

When the child reads material to you, use the same prompts to support the development of reading comprehension.

How is *your* comprehension? Let's do a little role-playing and try out a few comprehension prompts and strategies.

Tutors Know! *Reading Comprehension:* understanding what we read ourselves. Listening Comprehension: understanding what someone else reads to us!

Exercise #23: Background Experience

Your trainer will show you something to read. The experience will impress you with the important role that our personal experience brings to our ability to understand what we read.

1. What happened when you first read the selection? How did that change when you saw the title of the selection? What does this mean for our students and their ability to comprehend what they read?

2. Let's try it again with another selection. This time your trainer will prepare you for the reading, give you some background knowledge, and ask questions to help you understand the content. Record the comprehension *prompts* that are used before, during, and after the reading. A prompt is a question or inquiry that initiates the comprehension process.

   Before reading: ______

   During reading: ______

   After reading: ______

3. Tell about your experience with comprehension *this* time. How was it different from the first reading? Which reading example were you most comfortable with as a learner?

4. What other clues do authors provide for us that can be used to prepare young readers for what they will be reading?

How to Teach It: Comprehension

Predict, Apply, Retell

You will learn how to use three strategies to help your students improve their reading comprehension:

- Predict
- Apply background knowledge (previous experience)
- Retell

These strategies are typically used before reading, during reading, and after reading. Each one has prompts or questions associated with it.

Predict:

- "Tell me what you think will happen in this story."
- "What do you think will happen next?"

Apply Background Knowledge:

- "Tell me what you know about *(fill in the blank with something from the reading selection)*."
- "Has this every happened to you?"

Retell:

- "Tell me all about what you just read."
- "Tell me two things that you learned from your reading."

Key Point: As a tutor, your role will be to hold students accountable for reading for meaning. The simple questions and prompts that you use will send the message that when we read, we read to learn something! It is important to read for meaning and to remember!

Tutors Know! Tutors ask simple questions and talk about text meaning to help children understand that we read to learn!

Exercise #24

Do this activity with a partner. Consider the strategies above to answer these questions.

1. Which questions or prompts could you use *before reading*?

2. Which questions or prompts could you use *while the student is reading*?

3. Which questions or prompts could you use *when the student has finished reading*?

Share and discuss your answers with the group.

Practice It: Comprehension

You have learned three strategies that will form the basis for your focus on improving comprehension skills. Recall that comprehension is not an easy skill to teach because of the many language and processing skills that we use to gain meaning from text. The following activity will give you the opportunity to practice with your partner. You will work together to develop the prompts for each of the three strategies. Then, each of you will take a turn being the tutor or the student to try out the comprehension questions that you developed.

Read through each story together. Work together to develop your comprehension plan. Indicate whether your prompts will be used before, during, or after reading.

Story #1: Fooling Around

Rain and Wind sat resting on a mountain top. The sun was out, and there wasn't a cloud in the sky. Wind and Rain could see the people in the small town at the bottom of the mountain. Kids were playing in the park. People were sitting in the sun reading the Sunday paper. Everyone seemed happy.

Wind and Rain began to get bored because they didn't have anything to do. Wind said, "See me make the people run." Then Wind sent hats and papers flying down the street. Wind laughed, "What fun!"

Rain said, "I can make the people run too." So, Rain made black clouds. Soon big drops of water began falling. Rain laughed as the people ran for shelter.

(continued) **Story #1:** Fooling Around

Now develop two prompts for each strategy. For each prompt, indicate if you will use it before, during, or after reading the story.

Predict:

1. ______________________________

____

____

2. ______________________________

____

____

Apply Background Knowledge:

1. ______________________________

____

____

2. ______________________________

____

____

Retell:

1. ______________________________

____

____

2. ______________________________

____

____

Story #2: A Chicken's Life

Every chicken begins life the same way—as an egg. This is what happens. A hen and rooster mate. The hen lays between seven and fifteen eggs. Then the hen sits on the eggs until they hatch.

Once the hen lays the eggs, little chicks begin to form inside each of the eggs. At the start, the chicks seem to be little red specks on the eggs. In time, the specks get bigger.

After two days, you can see the heads of the chicks forming. After seven days, you can see the beginnings of their legs and wings. The chicks keep developing. Soon you can see their beaks. All this time, the mother hen sits on her nest.

After twenty-one days in the eggs, the little chicks run out of food. They become so big that they need to get out of their shells. "Peck, peck, peck."

All chicks have a tooth, called an egg tooth. The egg tooth helps them crack their shells. When they get out, the chicks are dripping wet and not very pretty. After a short time they fluff up. Soon they can eat and get around by themselves. "Cheep, cheep, cheep." Before long, the little chicks become roosters and hens.

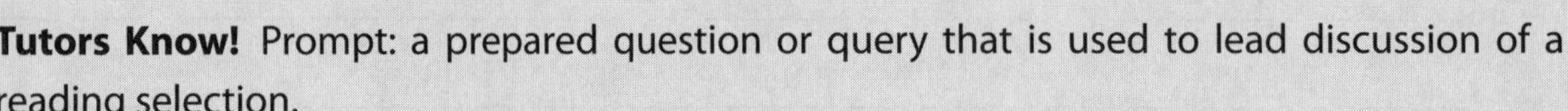
Tutors Know! Prompt: a prepared question or query that is used to lead discussion of a reading selection.

Now develop two prompts for each strategy. Indicate for each prompt if you will use it before, during, or after reading the story.

Predict:

1. ______________________________

____

____

2. ______________________________

____

____

(continued) **Story #2:** A Chicken's Life

Apply Background Knowledge:

1. ______________________________

2. ______________________________

Retell:

1. ______________________________

2. ______________________________

Share your prompts with the group. How do they compare? Do you hear other prompts that you would like to use? Write them here:

____

Use your prepared prompts to role-play student and tutor. When you are the tutor, record student successes and/or any concerns you may have with your student's responses.

Error Response

If your student is having difficulty with comprehension try the following:

- Model or show the student your thinking out loud as you answer the question or prompt. Then, ask the student to respond again: "Now you try." Ask the question again.
- On your data sheet, note the difficulty your student is having and share this information with your supervising teacher. Ask if there is anything else the teacher would like you to do during your tutor sessions to help improve comprehension.

Data Recording

Comprehension—*(circle one)* **Listening or Reading**

Student does this well: *(circle)*

predicts, applies background knowledge, retells

Student has difficulty with / I had to help the student with:

Discuss your teaching comprehension experiences with your group and trainer. Your trainer will help you prepare for the chapter assessment.

Review: Comprehension

1. What are three comprehension strategies that you can use to increase reading comprehension?

2. At what times during a student's reading will you apply your comprehension instruction?

3. What is the difference between listening comprehension and reading comprehension?

4. What is a prompt? Give three examples of prompts, one for each strategy covered in the lesson.

(continued) **Review:** Comprehension

5. How will you respond if your student has difficulty or makes an error? ____________________

Tutor's Tips

In this section you will find advice on how to *build positive relationships* with students, improve your *communication* with supervising teachers, and *organize* your student materials and time, as well as general tips to improve your instruction methods. You will also find ready-to-copy tutor *Strategy Reference Cards* for each of the five component areas you learned about. The data forms, phonics grids, etc., that you used during your training are also available in this section for you to copy.

Building and Maintaining Positive Relationships with Your Students

The relationships you establish with your students will contribute to the outcomes of your work with them. Building a sense of trust, safety, and security at the outset of your work with a child is critical to creating an environment where he or she feels comfortable taking risks. Chances are pretty good that the students with whom you will work have experienced reading failure in the past, which results in poor self-esteem and low confidence with reading tasks. They probably avoid reading because of repeated efforts to get better, without improvement. This can be a challenge for both the tutor and student at the start of a tutoring relationship. Here are some tips to help you get off to a positive start by building a safe and secure environment where students will be more open to taking risks and thus to becoming confident learners.

Set the Stage—Introduce Yourself

Start by introducing yourself. Talk about who you are, what you do for recreation, and your favorite foods. Show pictures of your family and pets. As you share these things about yourself, draw the student into the conversation: "Do you have a pet?" "Tell me about your family." "If you could have one wish for anything what would you wish? Why?" Help them to understand that you really care about what you do and about helping them learn to read. "We are going to have to work really hard sometimes. I will work hard to help you, and I need you to work hard too. But I will never ask you to do something that I have not prepared you to do, and I will be right here to help you."

Be Specific With Your Praise!

Sometimes, "Good job!" and "Excellent!" can lose their meaning. *Try to give specific praise that describes what the student did.* Here are some responses to a sampling of correct and incorrect student responses:

Phonemic Awareness Lesson

Student's Work	Tutor's Response
Student segments the sounds in a word correctly.	"Wow! You heard each of the sounds in that word and showed them to me."
Student gets stuck on segmenting the sounds in a word or does the task incorrectly.	"I heard you say the first and second sounds right." (Repeat them.) "Let me show you all of the sounds." (Do it for the student, and then have student do it alone.)
Student says he is bored with the lesson that you have prepared and are delivering.	"I know this seems boring to you, but let's get through it so that I can listen to you read!" Or: "Let's go through it quickly so we can move on." (Then pick up the pace.)
Student responses are all correct.	"I noticed that you were really paying attention during that part. You got them all right!"

Phonics Lesson

Student's Work	Tutor's Response
Student taps the letter sounds in her words and reads the words correctly.	"Great tapping those sounds! That helped you figure out the word."
Student guesses at the word and reads it incorrectly.	"The first sound was right on that word. Listen while I tap it." (Tap the word.) "Now you tap it with me. We'll come back to that one again later."
Student spells a word correctly.	"Way to match those sounds and letters! I can tell that you are getting better!"
Student spells a word incorrectly.	"The first part of the word is spelled right. Let me show you the right spelling." (Spell it, say the sounds and letters out loud, and underline or highlight the corrected parts. Have the student compare and trace your work, saying it as he spells it.) "When we say it as we spell it, it helps us remember. I bet you'll remember it next time!"

Fluency Lesson

Student's Work	Tutor's Response
Student improves his time on the second reading.	"I noticed that you were really concentrating during that reading. Look how far you read!"
Student does poorly on the first reading or worse on the second reading.	"Wow, that seemed hard for you. Let's read it together." (Read it aloud with the student, having the student follow with a marker or his finger.) "Now, try it again!" (If student still struggles, the passage may be too hard. Find an easier reading level.)

Vocabulary Lesson

Student's Work	Tutor's Response
Student uses a Wonder Word incorrectly.	"I can see how you would think that is a correct use for that word. Let me use it in a sentence for you." Or: "Tell me more to show you know the meaning."
Student uses a Wonder Word correctly.	"That is a great way to use the word ___________!"
Student illustrates the word.	"Great way to show you know the meaning of ________. Tell me about your picture and use the word again."

Comprehension Lesson

Student's Work	Tutor's Response
Student provides an appropriate response to an inquiry.	"You were really thinking while you were reading! Great way to tell about what you read."
Student does not respond correctly or does not know the answer to your question.	"I can see that you are trying to remember what you read. Let's read this part again and see if we can come up with a good answer."
At the end of the tutoring session:	"Thank you for your hard work today. I can tell that you are improving by how many words you read right today." Or: "I can tell that you are improving by how often I got to see your bright cheery smile!"

Organization

Keeping yourself organized can be a challenge! Here are some tips to help you:

- Create a three-ring notebook for each of your students in which to organize materials. Have the students create a colorful cover for their notebook.
- Create sections in the notebook for each of the five components and for data forms. Use these sections to compile your teaching tools and collect examples of the student's work.
- Review the lesson and prepare materials before you work with the student. This sounds pretty elementary, but to do it takes time and planning!
- Keep a notepad in each student notebook for the purpose of recording questions, student observations, and general comments that you will use as a guide for communicating with your supervising teacher.

Communication

Sometimes it is hard for tutors to know when to initiate communication with supervisors, to recognize and then communicate what is needed, or even what to say to them! Keep these tips in mind right from the start:

- Identify the individual who will be the main contact person for questions and guidance.
- Do not hesitate to ask questions!
- Arrange a regular weekly meeting time with the contact person and decide with him/her what the purpose of your meetings will be. This meeting content could include a review of student data, setting goals, a preview of upcoming lessons, the opportunity to express explicit and general impressions of how the sessions are progressing, and a discussion of responses to behavioral issues.
- Confidentiality—Keep in mind at all times that the students with whom you work are protected under privacy and confidentiality codes. Do not discuss your students with anyone except your main contact person or other teachers who work with the students. Limit these discussions to the

content of their reading lessons, their progress, and how to improve your instruction. Protect the students' notebooks and other data-collection materials. Respect families and individuals as you would want others to respect you and your family members.

Additional Tips

Instructional and interpersonal tips gleaned from the experience of veteran paraeducators and teachers are included in this section. Instructional tips are arranged by reading component to allow easy reference as the need arises for a new and different way to practice a skill! You may want to add some of these to your Strategy Reference Cards (available later in the workbook).

General

- Keep a variety of items available that you can use as manipulatives for phoneme lessons. Fish and teddy-bear crackers, one-inch blocks, colored paper squares, colored discs from math kits, dry beans, and flat beads are a few of the items you could keep in reclosable bags.

- Always have a couple of books at hand to read to the student. There may be times when the child doesn't feel well, or she may earn a special moment with you, or you may have extra time. Use these times to read to the child. Take advantage of the situation and apply some of your vocabulary and comprehension activities to improve listening comprehension.

- Provide an agenda for students. List the planned lesson components and the amount of time you intend to devote to each on a white board or sheet of paper. Let the student check off the components as you finish them. This can be extremely helpful with students who like to know what's expected of them.

Phonemic Awareness

Remember that with any phoneme activity, students acquire awareness of the phonemes in words in a predictable sequence. They begin by isolating the first sounds, then the last sounds, and then they develop the more difficult ability to isolate middle sounds in words. At the same time students are developing this awareness,

they are learning to do *complete segmentation* with words (/m//a//n/) and *blending* (hearing /m//a//n/ and saying *man*).

Games

Develop game boards to practice phonemic awareness. Bingo, concentration, and tic-tac-toe are three good games to start with. Use pictures instead of words on the game boards. Students match pictures that have the same initial, ending, or middle sounds, whichever you instruct them to listen for. Ask your supervising teacher for a good source of pictures to choose from.

Eat Your Words!

1. Say a word containing two to four sounds. Have students move small crackers into a line, one for each sound, saying the sounds as they separate out all of the sounds in the word.

2. Instruct the student to "Eat the /s/" or "Eat the /m/."

3. Push away the crackers and do another word.

Simple Warm-ups

- **Robot Talk**—This is an exercise for auditory blending. Say a word *segmented* with every phoneme separated by about a second of time. The students then repeat the word back to you, blending the sounds as a whole unit. Use words from your lesson: "/s/ /t/ /r/ /ee/ /t/... *street*!"

- **Thumbs up! Thumbs Down!**—Students are asked to put their thumbs up when they hear a given sound in the word that the teacher says. Thumbs go down if the sound is not present.

  "Listen for the sound /o͞o/, like in *moon*." Say several words, some with /o͞o/, such as *spoon*, *loon*, *boom*, *coop*, and others without the /o͞o/ sound. Students put their thumbs up when they hear words with the /o͞o/ sound. Say the word and the sound together as a group after the thumbs go up. "Spoon, /o͞o/."

- **Riddles**—Play this word activity with a focus on different phoneme positions.

  "I'm thinking of something good to eat. It *starts* with /p/." (pizza, pickles, pineapple)

  "I'm thinking of something in the room that *ends* with /r/. It is in your desk." (eraser, marker, sticker)

  "I'm thinking of someone's name that has the /ŏ/ sound *in* it." (Tom)

- **Make a Collection**—Begin this activity by telling the students that they are going to collect certain things today. The only things they can collect are things that start with a sound, end with a sound, or have a middle sound that you provide. (Use just one of the criteria.)

  "Let's start our collection with things that have a middle (vowel) sound /ă/." (cat, mat, fan, rat, can, etc.)

Phonics

Practice and Review with Simple Games

Play games that require a lot of reading of words from the students' lessons. Ideas for these games include:

- **Bingo**—Write words on flash cards and also randomly on a sheet of paper that has been divided into a 4 x 4 grid. You and the student take turns picking a card and reading it. A marker is placed on the word. First one to get a row filled reads the words back to you.

- **Concentration**—Make a set of flash cards with each word written on two cards. Deal the cards face down on the table. Take turns turning over a card, reading it, and then turning over a second card and reading it. If they match, the reader takes the cards. With young students, limit the number of words to around five (ten cards total) and use two different colors for the cards, say, green and blue. (Therefore, a green card would have a match with a blue card.)

- **Go Fish**—Use flash cards as playing cards. Write the words across the top so that when the child is holding the cards, the words are visible across the top. Or use a folder as a privacy screen, and allow students to lay out their cards on the table. "Do you have *cute*?" "Go fish!"

Construct Collections of Words from the Reading Program

These can be done on a poster or on colored paper that is placed in the student's notebook. Group words that share the same phonic element—for example, words that have the ow spelling. Review these regularly. Draw attention to the sound that the words share and then to the spelling.

Make a Word Book

Provide a simple book of stapled folded sheets of paper, and help students create their own word book. Students write the grapheme that you are introducing at the top of the page. After the lesson, students write words from the lesson that have the identified grapheme. Have them choose a word to illustrate to help them remember the sound that the grapheme makes. Students could also write sentences using the words.

Multisensory Experiences

Provide opportunities for students to see, hear, and touch letters in words. These activities can get students moving around and can vary the lesson to maintain attention.

- **Tracing**—This is a common multisensory practice. Students have a word written in front of them. Tracing with a pencil or crayon, students *see* each letter as they *say* the sound, as they *trace* the shape of the letter. Immediately after saying all of the sounds, they should blend the whole word.

- **Large Arm Movements**—Present a word visually, read it, then spell it in the air with large arm movements that start from the shoulder. Say each letter as it is created in the air. Then read the whole word.

- **Salt Tray**—Line a paper box lid with colored paper. Apply a thin layer of salt. Students draw letters as they say the letter names or sounds in the salt. Gently shake the lid to erase.

- **Waxed Pipe Cleaners**—Students can bend waxed pipe cleaners (available at craft and school supply stores) into letter shapes. These letter shapes will stick on slick surfaces such as desktops, windows, and notebook covers. Have students arrange the pipe-cleaner letters into words as you dictate them. Instruct students to use their finger to trace the letters in the words as the sounds or letter names are said aloud. Blend the whole word when done.

Flash Cards

The use of flash cards will probably be a mainstay of your teaching methods. There are several ways to get the most from flash cards. Remember these suggestions and practice them so that they become habit!

- Write words from your reading lessons on the flash cards. The words should represent sets that share the same phonic element—for example, all words with the silent-e pattern.
- Maintain a quick and lively pace! Hold the set in one hand with the front facing the student while your other hand moves the cards to the back of the deck or to another separate pile on the table. If your student does not automatically read the word, help him decode it and read it, and then move it to the back of the deck. "You'll see this word again in a minute!" You can also "hide" it somewhere in the middle of the pile. Student gets to keep all words that are read quickly and accurately in his own pile on the table. This makes a game out of a very effective practice tool.
- Hold the cards so that all students in a group see the words. Instruct students to read the words chorally, at the same time, by giving them a cue: "What word?" Vary this by occasionally calling on an individual. "Get ready… Joe. Get ready… Mary. Get ready… Everybody!" Keep the pace moving.
- Store flash cards in envelopes labeled with the phonic element represented by the words. Let students take them home to practice or to keep when they know them well.

Fluency

Repeated readings will be your most common method of fluency training. Here are a few other ideas to increase reading opportunities for your students.

- **Choral Reading**—Group reads together aloud.
- **Echo Reading**—Group reads aloud phrase-by-phrase or sentence-by-sentence, repeating after a live or taped model. Follow along in the text with a marker or with your finger.
- **Shared Reading**—Tutor reads aloud *with* the child, maintaining a steady fluent pace for the child to keep up with.

- **Partner Reading**—Student *takes turns* reading aloud with the tutor, who provides help with word identification and feedback. Each reader follows along as the other reads.

- **Auditory Modeling**—Students are given exposure to modeling of fluent reading. By listening to fluent reading, students learn how a reader's voice attends to punctuation, mood, and pacing.

Vocabulary

Play games with the Wonder Words that students collect.

- **I'm Thinking**—Choose several words from the students' collections. Ask riddle questions for students to answer.

  "I'm thinking of a word that I would use when I am really happy."

  "I'm thinking of a word that means the opposite of big."

- **Concentration**—Match words with their meanings. Create matching cards with the word on one card and the meaning, or a sentence using that word, on another card. Deal words together face down on one side of the work space and meanings face down on the other side of the work space. Students take turns trying to match words with meanings.

- **Game Board Vocabulary**—Write the Wonder Words on cards and place them in a box or bag. Have a student draw a card from the box or bag; if she can use the word on the card correctly in a sentence that shows she understands the meaning, she then rolls dice and moves on a game board.

Comprehension

- **Draw a Picture**—Discuss favorite parts of the reading. Provide students with paper and crayons and let them illustrate their favorite parts. Make sure that you have ample time for this activity. Instruct students to retell the favorite parts when they are through with their drawings.

- **Order the Story**—Rewrite the main parts of the story in brief sentences, one per strip of paper. Mix up the strips and instruct students to place the strips in order to retell the story.

- **Buddy Tell**—After reading, pair students. Instruct one student to tell the other student everything they remember about the story. When the student is finished, have the listening student to share any information that might have been left out.

Strategy Reference Cards

The teaching tools that you learned during your training are organized here in separate reproducible boxes. Laminate or print on stiff paper and place on a ring for handy reference as you teach. You may wish to add some of the previous Tutor's Tips to your collection!

Strategy Reference Card #1

Phonemic Awareness

Choose 10 single-syllable words from the student text.

- **Isolate Initial Sounds**—Say the word and ask student to say the word and the first sound in that word. Repeat the word and sound with the student.
- **Isolate Final Sounds**—Say the word and ask the student to say the word and the last sound in that word. Repeat the word and the sound with the student.
- **Isolate Middle Sounds**—Say the word and ask the student to say the word and the middle sound in that word. Repeat the word and the sound with the student. Make sure that the words you choose for this have a distinguishable middle sound; three-sound words work best. If a student has difficulty here, use markers to segment the word and have student identify and say the middle sound using the markers.
- **Complete Segmentation**—Say a word and ask student to tell you all of the little sounds in that word.
- **"Secret" Language (Auditory Blending)**—Say a word segmented into its isolated sounds, and ask the student to say the "secret word" back to you.

Strategy Reference Card #2

Phonemic Awareness–Segmentation

Multisensory Cues:

- ***Tap the Sounds***—Beginning with your index finger, tap once for each sound as you move through each finger.
- ***Tap Head, Waist, Ankles***—To help students isolate middle sounds, use three-sound words and tap your head for the first sound, your waist for the middle sound, and then reach down to your feet for the last sound.
- ***Finger Count***—Count and say the sounds one at a time, raising a finger for each one.
- ***Pull the Sounds Out of Your Mouth***—Starting at your lips, pretend to grasp each isolated sound as you move your thumb and forefinger in a pulling movement away from your mouth.
- ***Use Manipulatives***—Use little crackers, paper squares, or game pieces to help children see the segmentation as they separate the sounds in words.

Strategy Reference Card #3

Phonemic Awareness Data Recording

When you are teaching phonemic awareness, pay close attention to your students' responses. When errors are made, note what kinds of errors they are making:

- Are they able to do complete phoneme segmentation?
- Are they able to auditorially blend the phoneme-separated words that you give them?
- Are they confusing sounds? Example: saying /b/ for /p/, or /t/ for /d/.
- Do they consistently miss the last sounds or middle sounds in words?

Strategy Reference Card #4

Phonics–Whole-Word Blending

Another name for this procedure is "touch and say." Children touch each letter (or grapheme), say the sounds and then blend the sounds to read the word.

Step-by-step procedure for decoding shack:

1. Point to the digraph *sh* and say, "Sound"; students say "/sh/."
2. Point to the *a* and say, "Sound"; students say "/a/."
3. Point to the *ck* and say, "Sound"; students say "/k/."
4. Slide finger under the whole word to blend it; students say, "*Shack*".
5. Point to the word and say, "The word is *shack*."
6. Check for understanding of the word and the ability to use it in a sentence.

Strategy Reference Card #5

Phonics—Stretch-and-Say Blending

Phonemes are segmented and counted and then the whole word is blended with an accompanying gesture to pull the sounds together into the word.

Step-by-step procedure for decoding *sun*:

1. Say the whole word, "Sun."
2. Ask students to hold up one finger for each sound they hear as the word is segmented and the phonemes counted.
3. Say the whole word while pulling arm down or sweeping it across your body from left to right.

Strategy Reference Card #6

Phonics–Tap and Blend

This method is similar to Whole-Word Blending except that the student is actively involved with the decoding process through tapping the sounds as tutor and student work through the word together.

Step-by-step procedure for decoding *stick*:

In unison, tutor and student tap index finger and thumb together as they say each sound in the word and blend the sounds together. If needed, the tutor can touch each grapheme as the student taps the sounds.

1. Tap and say "/s/."
2. Tap and say "/t/."
3. Tap and say "/ĭ/."
4. Tap and say "/k/."
5. Run finger under whole word and say, "Stick."

Strategy Reference Card #7

Phonics–Sounds to Spelling

The student separates the sounds in a word and then applies the grapheme for those sounds. That is, the student spells the word.

You will need the following materials:

- Copies of the Sounds to Spelling form or a sheet of paper with boxes and lines.
- Moveable sound markers—paper squares or little crackers, some small items that the students can use to represent the separate phonemes.
- Words from the student's reading materials.

Step-by-step procedure for decoding *book*:

1. Tutor says, "Book."
2. Student repeats the word and moves markers into the spaces for each separate sound, saying the sounds as the markers are touched and moved—" /b/ /o͝o/ /k/."
3. The tutor asks two types of questions about the sounds: "Show me the /k/," and then, pointing to the second sound marker, "What is this sound?" Student says, "/o͝o/."

   These two questions can be repeated for different sounds in the word so that the student is responding to questions about all of the represented sounds.
4. Once the questions have been asked, the student is instructed to push up the markers one at a time and write the graphemes for each sound in the spaces, saying the sounds as the letters are written.
5. The student then writes the entire word on the line.

Strategy Reference Card #8

Phonics–Individual Letter Sounds

Materials: Moveable letters (letters written on flash cards or actual letter shapes).

1. "This letter *m* makes the sound /m/. Say it with me, /m/. What sound does the *m* (pointing) make?" "When we see *m* in a word, we say /m/."

Follow the same process for each letter, teaching the sounds.

2. Point randomly to the letters, asking for the sounds. Point and say, "What sound?" Keep a quick pace. Make it lively: "I am going to try to trick you…."

3. Ask the student to show you a given sound. "Show me the /s/. Show me the /ă/."

In the group of letters you are teaching, use 70% letter sounds the child knows and 30% letter sounds the child is learning.

Strategy Reference Card #9

Fluency–Repeated Readings

Materials: Stopwatch, a repeated readings chart, three different colored pencils or markers, a reading passage that is written at the child's instructional level, and a copy of the reading passage on which to mark errors.

Step-by-Step Process: Instruct the student: "Please read this passage for your fluency training today. Begin reading here (point), and read until I tell you to stop. If you come to a word you don't know, I will tell you the word." Time him for one minute, and note the number of words he reads. Subtract the errors for a total of words read correctly per minute (WCPM).

1. Chart the WCPM on the repeated readings chart. Show the student how to graph his own performance.

2. Review the errors with the student. Show and tell him the words you helped him with, words he omitted or substituted, and words he hesitated with.

3. Instruct the student to read the passage again, and follow the same procedure.

4. Do this for a total of three times marking the errors with a different color each time. Have student graph his performance after each reading. Work with the student to set goals between readings—"How many words can you read next time? Can you beat your time?"

Strategy Reference Card #10

Fluency–Repeated Readings: How do you know what text to use?

- If your students are just beginning to learn **letter sounds**, repeated readings are to be done with a page of letters from which letter sounds will be read.
- If your students are **decoding and blending single words** to practice building automaticity, do repeated readings with isolated words that reflect the target decoding skills you are working on.
- Once your students are reading **passages of text, such as paragraphs and stories**, use these texts for repeated readings. This level of repeated reading generally begins around mid-first grade.

Strategy Reference Card #11

Fluency–What To Count As Errors When Doing Repeated Readings

Errors:

- *Unknown word.* The student hesitates or attempts to read a word but does not produce the correct word in three seconds. Provide the correct word for the student and mark it as an error on your sheet.
- *Substitution.* The student misreads a word, substituting a different word for the actual word in the text.
- *Omission.* The student leaves a word out while reading.

Not Errors:

- Rereading words or phrases.
- Self-corrections made within three seconds.
- Skipping a line. (Do not count the words in the omitted line as errors.)

Strategy Reference Card #12

Vocabulary

Vocabulary instruction begins with finding **Wonder Words** in reading material that you will be reading to the students or material that they will be reading themselves. Follow these steps:

- Preread the material that your students will be reading or that you will read to your students.
- Choose two words that meet the Wonder Words criteria: a) words or phrases that may be difficult to understand and that the students may hear or read again and therefore need to know; or b) words that may have multiple meanings.
- Show the written Wonder Words to the students. Read the words. "These are Wonder Words that you will be reading today."
- Read each word and provide definitions.
- Tell about the word using the context of the story.
- Have the students record a picture or brief definition in their Wonder Words journal to help recall the meaning.
- Instruct the students to read the passage.

Strategy Reference Card #13

Vocabulary

Tip—Revisit students' **Wonder Words** journals and discuss the words in relation to a story. Always encourage students to use the Wonder Words in their discussion. "Tell me about it, and use the word _________." Rephrase for the students if they do not use the Wonder Words. Provide opportunities for the students to apply the vocabulary to their own experiences.

Strategy Reference Card #14

Comprehension

These strategies are typically used before reading, during reading, and after reading. Each one has its own prompt or question associated with it.

Predict:

- "Tell me what you think will happen later in this story."
- "What do you think will happen next?"

Apply Background Knowledge:

- "Tell me what you know about *(fill in the blank with something from the reading selection)*."
- "Has this ever happened to you?"

Retell:

- "Tell me all about what you just read."
- "Tell me two things that you learned from your reading."

Strategy Reference Card #15

Vocabulary and Comprehension Error Response

If your student is having difficulty with vocabulary or comprehension try the following:

- Model or show the student *your* thinking out loud as you answer the question or prompt. Then, ask the student to respond again: "Now you try." Ask the question again.
- On your data sheet, note the difficulty your student is having and share this information with your supervising teacher. Ask if there is anything else the teacher would like you to do during your tutor sessions to help improve vocabulary or comprehension.

Strategy Reference Card #16

General Error Response

1. Point out one thing that was done correctly.
2. Demonstrate the correct way.
3. Point out the place where a correction was made. Explain.
4. Have the student do it again, with you.

Note the error on your data form.

Forms

Forms and blackline masters for many of the teaching tools used in the *ParaReading* training are included in this section.

- **Data Forms**—Three different forms are included. Choose one of these forms to use if there is not a data form included with your reading program. Record what your students do well and any concerns that arise during your tutoring sessions.

- **Sounds to Spelling Form**—This is a phonics lesson form that makes it easy to segment words by applying graphemes to the sounds in a word.

- **Fluency Training: Repeated Readings Chart**—Here is a form that can be used for three sessions of repeated readings. Each session records three readings of the same material.

- **Wonder Words Journal**—Copy several of these two-sided, then fold and staple and add a colorful cover to create a Wonder Words journal.

- **Phonics Grids**—Students use the empty grid to write graphemes in as you dictate them, and then cut them out to build words. The completed grids can be used to review and to cut and build words. Note that you may have to add extras of some letters if words contain many of the same letters.

- **LETRS Consonant and Vowel Articulation Charts**—Use these charts to practice saying phonemes in the phonemic awareness chapter.

Data Form 1

Student Name: ______________________

Monday **Date:** **Comments:**	**Sounds**—*Student does well: (circle)* initial, ending, middle, segmentation, blending *Student errors: (circle)* initial, ending, middle, segmentation, blending **Decoding**—*Student errors: (circle)* specific letter-sound correspondences, whole-word blending, letter-sound confusion **Fluency**—*Record WCPM:* 1st reading ________ 2nd reading ________ 3rd Reading ________ **Vocabulary**—Can the student use the vocabulary words in a sentence that shows he/she knows the word? Yes No **Comprehension**—*Student does well:(circle)* predicts, applies background knowledge, retells
Tuesday **Date:** **Comments:**	**Sounds**—*Student does well: (circle)* initial, ending, middle, segmentation, blending *Student errors: (circle)* initial, ending, middle, segmentation, blending **Decoding**—*Student errors: (circle)* specific letter-sound correspondences, whole-word blending, letter-sound confusion **Fluency**—*Record WCPM:* 1st reading ________ 2nd reading ________ 3rd Reading ________ **Vocabulary**—Can the student use the vocabulary words in a sentence that shows he/she knows the word? Yes No **Comprehension**—*Student does well:(circle)* predicts, applies background knowledge, retells
Wednesday **Date:** **Comments:**	**Sounds**—*Student does well: (circle)* initial, ending, middle, segmentation, blending *Student errors: (circle)* initial, ending, middle, segmentation, blending **Decoding**—*Student errors: (circle)* specific letter-sound correspondences, whole-word blending, letter-sound confusion **Fluency**—*Record WCPM:* 1st reading ________ 2nd reading ________ 3rd Reading ________ **Vocabulary**—Can the student use the vocabulary words in a sentence that shows he/she knows the word? Yes No **Comprehension**—*Student does well:(circle)* predicts, applies background knowledge, retells
Thursday **Date:** **Comments:**	**Sounds**—*Student does well: (circle)* initial, ending, middle, segmentation, blending *Student errors: (circle)* initial, ending, middle, segmentation, blending **Decoding**—*Student errors: (circle)* specific letter-sound correspondences, whole-word blending, letter-sound confusion **Fluency**—*Record WCPM:* 1st reading ________ 2nd reading ________ 3rd Reading ________ **Vocabulary**—Can the student use the vocabulary words in a sentence that shows he/she knows the word? Yes No **Comprehension**—*Student does well:(circle)* predicts, applies background knowledge, retells
Friday **Date:** **Comments:**	**Sounds**—*Student does well: (circle)* initial, ending, middle, segmentation, blending *Student errors: (circle)* initial, ending, middle, segmentation, blending **Decoding**—*Student errors: (circle)* specific letter-sound correspondences, whole-word blending, letter-sound confusion **Fluency**—*Record WCPM:* 1st reading ________ 2nd reading ________ 3rd Reading ________ **Vocabulary**—Can the student use the vocabulary words in a sentence that shows he/she knows the word? Yes No **Comprehension**—*Student does well:(circle)* predicts, applies background knowledge, retells

Data Form 2

Student Name: ____________________

Record student performance, data, and notes to communicate with student's teacher.

Week of:	**Week of:**	**Week of:**	**Week of:**
Phonemic Awareness:	Phonemic Awareness:	Phonemic Awareness:	Phonemic Awareness:
Phonics:	Phonics:	Phonics:	Phonics:
Fluency:	Fluency:	Fluency:	Fluency:
Vocabulary and Comprehension:	Vocabulary and Comprehension:	Vocabulary and Comprehension:	Vocabulary and Comprehension:

Data Form 3

Student Name: ______________________

Record student performance, data, and notes to communicate with student's teacher.

	MONDAY	TUESDAY	WEDNESDAY	THURSDAY	FRIDAY
Phonemic Awareness					
Decoding/Phonics					
Fluency					
Comprehension Vocabulary					

Sounds to Spelling

Student Name: ____________________

____

____

____

____

Fluency Training: Repeated Readings Chart

Student Name: ______________________________

Words Read Correctly Per Minute	Date: ______________ Reading Selection: ______________ ______________	Date: ______________ Reading Selection: ______________ ______________	Date: ______________ Reading Selection: ______________ ______________	
120				120
100				100
90				90
80				80
70				70
60				60
50				50
40				40
30				30
20				20
10				10
0				0
	1 2 3	1 2 3	1 2 3	

Wonder Words

Wonder Words

Grid One

Grid One Completed

a apple	e echo	i itch	o octopus	u up		
a-e babe	i-e hive	o-e rose	u-e tube	u-e mule	e-e theme	
m man	p pump	s sun	b boy	t tame	d dog	f fun
l lap	r rabbit	n nose	w wish	h hair	c cat	k kite
j jam	g goat	g gym	c city	y yummy	v valentine	z zipper
qu quilt	x box					
ir shirt	er sister	ur burp	ar arm	or corn		
au autumn	aw awesome	ai sail	ay day	ee bee	oa boat	oi oil
oy joy	ea See LETRS Vowel Chart	ou See LETRS Vowel Chart	ow See LETRS Vowel Chart	oo See LETRS Vowel Chart	ew chew	
th thin	th them	sh shoe	ch chin	ng ring		

Grid Two

o	u	i	a			
n	b	g	l	s	m	p
th	ng	sh				
aw	oo	ur	ee			
f	t					
r	c					

LETRS Vowel Chart

ē	see, these, me, eat, key, happy, chief, either
ĭ	sit, gym
ā	make, rain, play, great, baby, eight, vein, they
ĕ	bed, breath
ă	cat
ī	time, pie, cry, right, rifle
ŏ	fox, swap, palm
ŭ	cup, cover, flood, tough
aw	saw, pause, call, water, bought
ō	vote, boat, toe, snow, open, go
o͝o	took, put, could
ū	moo, tube, blue, chew, suit, soup
yū	cute, few, universe
ə	about, lesson, elect, definition, circus
oi/oy	oil, boy
ou/ow	out, cow
er	her, fur, sir
ar	cart
or	sport

Consonant Phonemes by Place and Manner of Articulation

	Lips	Teeth/ Lips	Tongue/ Teeth	Ridge/ Teeth	Roof Mouth	Back of Throat	Glottis
Stops (Unvoiced / Voiced)	/p/ /b/			/t/ /d/		/k/ /g/	
Nasals	/m/			/n/		/ng/	
Fricatives (Unvoiced / Voiced)		/f/ /v/	/th/ /th/	/s/ /z/	/sh/ /zh/		
Affricates (Unvoiced / Voiced)					/ch/ /j/		
Glides (Unvoiced / Voiced)					/y/	/wh/ /w/	/h/
Liquids				/l/ /r/			

The Trainer's Manual

Welcome to the Trainer

Welcome to the fun and rewarding world of training reading tutors! Paraeducators are a valuable resource for schools and private learning centers, where improving the reading skills of our young children is a priority. No Child Left Behind necessitates that we teach all children to read to ensure that the world of knowledge and opportunity is open to everyone. It is imperative that we place qualified tutors with our students who are at risk for reading failure. This manual will guide and support paraeducator training and will make clear the basics of *what* to teach to make students competent readers and *how* to teach it.

This introduction will explain how the content of *ParaReading* is organized, provide suggested timelines for the training, and recommend how best to implement your *ParaReading* training program to optimize your training efforts.

Trainer's Text

Organization

- *ParaReading* is designed to be a complete tutor and tutor trainer manual. The Paraeducator's Workbook comprises the front section of *ParaReading*, and the back section contains the Trainer's Manual.
- The Trainer's Manual is set up to correspond by page number to the Paraeducator's Workbook, with the addition of trainer notes and directions. Therefore, when the participants are on page 25 in the workbook, the trainer will be on page T25 in the trainer's section, where additional information and directions guide instruction, explain how to lead activities, and synthesize information for the trainer.
- Additional tutor advice and data forms are in the Tutor's Tips section at the end of the Paraeducator's Workbook. The forms can be copied and used by the tutors when their training is completed.
- Lesson directions in the Trainer's Manual provide transparency numbers and titles, step-by-step activity directions, and time estimates to help trainers plan and utilize the training materials and structure their training time efficiently and effectively. (The amount of time for a lesson is

indicated only when there is a structured presentation or an exercise for paraeducators to perform.)

Timelines

The training can be delivered following one or a combination of schedule options to meet the needs of schools, districts, and individuals involved. Recommendations include:

- Training one component at a time. Allow approximately three hours per component for a relaxed training atmosphere with thorough material coverage.
- Training over two full days. The material can be covered adequately in this time period; however, consider offering a follow up at a later date to review and strengthen the material and to cover the information in the Tutor's Tips section.
- Training that is customized to meet predetermined needs or weak component areas. If schools choose this option, we recommend that the Phonemic Awareness and Phonics components be offered in the order presented and that neither one be omitted from the training.

Optimize Training Efforts

Preparation

- Preview the *ParaReading* lessons to get a sense of each chapter's organization. Read the Paraeducator's Workbook, and then read the Trainer's Manual, which provides step-by-step instructions for teaching the content. Highlight main ideas and details in the Trainer's Manual for quick reference during the training.
- Complete the Paraeducator's Workbook prior to teaching it. This will give you hands-on experience with the tasks that will be asked of the participants.
- Make overhead transparencies from the blackline masters. Place them in protector sheets in a notebook organized by component for use during training.
- Gather and prepare all activity materials (see the Materials List later in this section).

Effective Training

- Provide *name tags* for the participants. Use their first names when calling on them, requesting feedback, or pointing out exceptional work. Learn their names and make an effort to talk with them individually during breaks and while monitoring the room during independent activities.

- Keep a steady and lively *pace* throughout the training sessions. Have your materials ready and move through the discussions and activities at a pace that allows participants to feel unhurried and that respects the time they need to assimilate, review, and practice new information.

- *Greet* participants as the class assembles, and ask a few of the more gregarious types if they wouldn't mind helping out as volunteers for some of the activities. Communicate that it is OK if they do not feel comfortable volunteering. Observe the class for individuals who appear to be comfortable with the content, and call on them by name when participation is needed.

- Prepare for the activities. Most of the activities are designed to *scaffold learning*. This means that activities direct the trainer to first demonstrate an activity or concept, then do it together with the participants, and then, finally, to let the participants practice independently. This "I do it, we do it, you do it" model is critical to the design of the training.

- Announce a training *schedule* including breaks at the beginning of each training session. Several quick breaks can help keep attention levels high. Time the breaks, and adhere to the schedule!

- Provide edible *treats* to reward and maintain interest. Participants may wish to sign up to contribute treats for the group when there are multiple sessions scheduled.

Assessing Tutors After Each Component

All participants are assessed using the chapter reviews following each component. This is an important element of *ParaReading*.

- Prepare tutors for the assessment reviews through an oral review of the material first, then instruct them to complete the assessments independently.

- The assessment reviews will assist in determining if individuals have mastered the content and are ready to apply their knowledge when tutoring. Mastery levels should be 90% to 100% on all components.
- The assessment reviews will enable schools to report levels of qualified paraeducators who are tutoring reading in their schools.

Answer these questions before training begins:

- What will the process be for correcting the assessments?
- What will the process be for reassessing if a paraeducator does not meet criteria of 90% to 100% accuracy?

Recommendations for Paraeducators Who Do Not Meet Criteria:

- Paraeducator attends another training session.
- Paraeducator is observed while tutoring and provided with feedback and modeling as necessary and is then reassessed
- Paraeducator receives individualized one-on-one or small-group review of the information and is then reassessed.

Important:

Discuss the predetermined assessment procedure with participants at the beginning of the training. It is important that participants are fully aware of the process that will be followed with the paraeducators who do not meet mastery criteria on the component assessments. Make this a nonthreatening discussion; assure participants that your intention is for all paraeducators to become highly qualified and that you will work closely with them to ensure that their levels of learning are high.

Materials List

Materials needed for Chapter 1: Phonemic Awareness

- Name tags
- *Transparencies and overhead markers
- A set of the Strategy Reference Cards (Tutor's Tips section) on a ring
- Paper and crayons or colored markers
- Pushpins or tape for mounting pictures to wall
- Fish crackers or other small moveable objects
- Pocket mirrors
- Chart paper and marker

Materials needed for Chapter 2: Phonics

- Name tags
- Handout copies of p. 35 and p. 36
- *Transparencies and overhead markers
- 3" x 5" cards or self-stick notes for decoding practice
- Paper to be used for making response cards—each participant will need a half sheet
- Scissors
- Manipulatives to use as markers—suggestions: fish crackers, hard candies, popcorn
- Grapheme letter tiles (Grid Two) cut out of transparency film
- Zippered plastic sandwich bags to put letters in

Materials needed for Chapter 3: Fluency

- Name tags
- *Transparencies and overhead markers
- A decodable or other child's text to demonstrate fluency and disfluency
- Three different-colored pencils or pens
- Stopwatch

Materials needed for Chapter 4: Vocabulary

- Name tags
- *Transparencies and overhead markers
- Scissors
- Chart paper
- Pictures for processor exercise cut from transparency film

Materials needed for Chapter 5: Comprehension

- Name tags
- *Transparencies and overhead markers

*See the Blackline Masters section for transparency masters.

ParaReading Class Roster, Assessment Record

Training Date: ____________ Location: ____________ Trainer: ____________

Record Performance and General Comments:

Tutor Name	Phonemic Awareness Review & Segmentation	Phonics Review & Nonsense Words	Fluency Review	Vocabulary Review	Comprehension Review

Welcome to the Paraeducator

Welcome to *ParaReading*. This paraeducator training will prepare you to be a confident, knowledgeable reading tutor who is available to help children, their families, and the personnel with whom you work. Children benefit from the relationships you build with them because students who work one on one with caring tutors demonstrate improved self-esteem and confidence (Wasik, 1998; Fitzgerald, 2001). Families profit when their children who are at risk of academic failure begin to succeed and gain confidence as learners. And schools and learning centers need paraeducators to provide the needed manpower to reach all children. As a paraeducator, you are a very valuable person and perform a very important role. The goals (broad-based learning) and objectives (action-oriented, observable outcomes) for your *ParaReading* training are listed below.

Goals

Effective paraeducators:

- Understand the important roles that phonemic awareness, phonics (or decoding), fluency, vocabulary, and comprehension have in reading instruction.
- Learn how to apply systematic and direct practices to teach students the five basic components of reading.
- Acquire specific instructional, record-keeping, and tutorial management skills.

Objectives

Effective paraeducators:

- Observe modeling of instructional techniques and instructional content and participate in role-playing during the training.
- Demonstrate mastery of the explicit systematic learning that strengthens effective reading instruction.
- Deliver praise, encouragement, positive feedback, and reinforcement as part of their successful instruction.

Trainer Presentation: 15 min.

Lesson Emphasis: Participants are welcomed and introduced to the training goals.

1. Tell participants that they are valuable. You are honored to be training them for a very important task—teaching children to read.
2. Direct a discussion. Ask participants why they are present at the training. What do they expect to learn from the training? Establish expectations for the training.

Transparency 1
***ParaReading* Training Goals**

Transparencies 2-3
Objectives

3. Read the goals and objectives, and compare the goals and objectives with the participants' expectations.
4. Tell participants that it is very important to ensure that they are qualified to instruct reading. Therefore, the training has an assessment/review process. Explain that at the end of each component chapter there will be a review that assesses their mastery of the content. Participants are bound to be nervous or apprehensive about the assessment. Assure them that their doing well with the assessment is your highest priority and that you will prepare them for taking it.
5. Explain the process chosen by your school that will be followed when tutors do not meet 90% to 100% mastery (see Assessing Tutors After Each Component earlier in the manual).

Trainer Presentation: 10 min.

Lesson Emphasis: Five components form the basic foundation for the *ParaReading* training: Phonemic Awareness, Phonics (or Decoding), Fluency, Vocabulary, and Comprehension.

Transparency 4
Star with Components

1. Tell participants briefly about the National Reading Panel's task of reviewing scientific research and that the five guiding components that are the outcomes of that analysis—phonemic awareness, phonics, fluency, vocabulary, and comprehension—provide the basis for the training, for our assessment of students' skills, and for our reading instruction. Point to each component on the star as you list them.
2. Explain that the training also teaches a process for data collection, what to do when students make mistakes, how to communicate with supervising teachers, and how to build positive relationships with students.
3. Show participants your ring of Strategy Reference Cards; they will make one of these at the end of the training. It will help participants remember and apply what they have learned!

ParaReading
A Training Guide for Tutors

- Recognize areas in which students need extra help, and understand the importance of communicating observations to supervisors when there are questions or concerns.
- Utilize error-correction procedures that are quick, simple, and consistently applied.
- Keep accurate records as an assessment of a student's progress, of their work, and for program evaluation.

ParaReading Training

Content

ParaReading training is based upon five critical components of reading instruction. These components can be illustrated as five points on a star:

To further strengthen your training, suggestions for data collection, organization, how to respond to student errors, and communication with supervising teachers are included in the Tutor's Tips section of this workbook, along with additional instructional advice. In the Tutor's Tips section, you will also find Strategy Reference Cards, the tutor strategies that you learn in this training formatted for use as a quick teaching reference!

10

Format

The Paraeducator's Workbook presents each of the five reading components in its own chapter designed to help you become familiar with the component and how to teach it. Your lessons will follow this consistent format:

- **Discussion**—Each chapter begins with a discussion of the focus component. Your trainer will present background information and research, so that you will understand the importance of the skill being taught.
- **Your Turn to Learn**—Your Turn to Learn provides opportunities for you to practice and perfect your own reading skills in the area of focus. Paraeducators may have their skills assessed during this section.
- **How to Teach It**—Procedures for teaching the focus skill are presented in this section. Necessary instructional materials are listed, and a data collection process is described.
- **Practice It**—Before you teach any reading skill, you should have lots of practice! The training allows time to observe, practice in pairs, and role-play with other tutors and the trainer.
- **Review**—A brief review assessment completes each chapter. These reviews are meant to provide helpful feedback to you and your trainer as you progress through the training.

> **Note to the Paraeducator** When we teach, it is natural to assume that our students will learn using the same methods and tools that *our* teachers used when we were learning. It is important to put aside your memories of how you learned and even how your own children learned as you begin this training. Research provides the key to helping us design and deliver instruction that works for the majority of kids at risk (Foorman, Francis, Fletcher, Schatschneider, & Mehta 1998; Moats, 1999). *ParaReading* uses this research as the basis for training you to implement effective, proven reading practices. Good luck! You are on your way to becoming a *ParaReading* tutor and to giving the gift of reading to the children you teach!

Trainer Presentation: 5 min.

Lesson Emphasis: Participants will understand the training lesson format used to introduce and teach each of the five components. To emphasize the importance of the work they do to teach reading, participants will consider a student with whom they have worked.

Transparency 5
***ParaReading* Lesson Format**

1. Present the lesson format. Read and discuss each section and its purpose.
2. Ask a volunteer to read the "Note to the Paraeducator." Explain that we have clear substantive information on how children learn to read. This is the information that they will learn in this training and apply to reading instruction.

Complete the Exercise: 15 min.

Materials—8" x 10" paper, colored markers, push pins or tape for mounting on wall.

1. Tell participants to draw their images following directions on this page and write answers to the questions on the next page.
2. Ask for volunteers to share something about their person. Ask these questions to lead a discussion:
   - "Tell about why you chose this person."
   - "Tell about an event you recall that illustrates the difficulty this person had with learning to read."
3. Lead the discussion about these individuals to capture the discouragement, emotional issues, and desire to teach and improve the lives of individuals who struggle with reading.
4. Post the pictures around the room: "This is our class; these are our students as we learn."

   Note: Refer to this "class" when appropriate during the training. Get to know these individuals—"If Joey had difficulty with isolating first sounds in a word, what do we do?"

ParaReading
A Training Guide for Tutors

Exercise: Before We Begin

Consider your previous encounters with a child who had difficulty learning to read. Who comes to mind? A boy or a girl? How old? What were some of this child's experiences with learning to read?

Use colored markers and a piece of paper to draw the person you're thinking of. It doesn't have to be a work of art ready to hang in a museum; the critical thing here is that you create an image of the person who will represent why you want to learn how to effectively help children improve their reading.

Write about your person:

1. Tell about why you chose this person.
2. Tell about an event you recall that illustrates the difficulty this person had with learning to read.

Post your drawing in an area of the room set aside by your trainer. Look at all of the pictures of all of the children. Imagine that they are your students while you learn *ParaReading*!

Chapter 1: Phonemic Awareness

Discussion

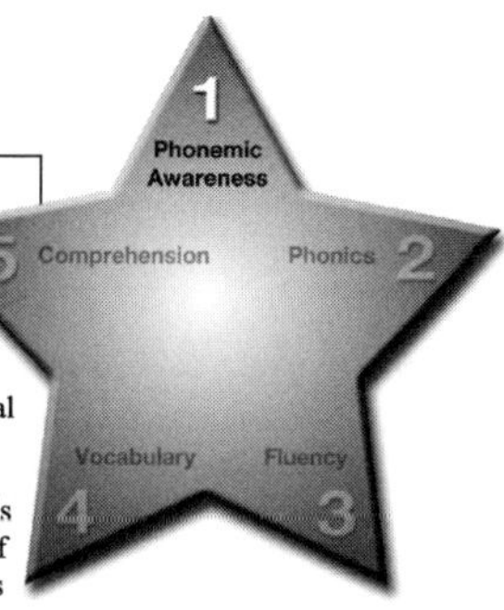

Exercise #1: Listen and respond as your trainer asks you to answer some simple word-play tasks.

The tasks that you just completed require a linguistic skill called *phonemic awareness*. Phonemic awareness happens in the absence of visual letters. The listener's focus is on oral language, on speech sounds.

The ability to separate and produce speech sounds in words requires one to have phonemic awareness, or awareness of the speech sounds in one's own language. This ability seems simple to us, yet to many young children the questions you were asked are not easy to answer. Phonemic awareness is one of the critical skills that enable young children to decode written language into spoken language and read!

If you ask a young child who is preparing to enter first grade, "What are you going to learn in school?", the answer will invariably be, "I am going to learn to read!" First grade is where we gain entrance into the world of reading. School is where we learn to read. Reading is what opens worlds to us; reading is what older brothers and sisters, friends, and parents can do, and, now, "I am going to learn to read too!"

Unfortunately, though, reading does not come easily to about 40% of children (Vellutino & Scanlon, 1987). They watch anxiously as others in their class begin to make sense of those letters on a page, while it remains a struggle to them. Slowly, over time, if they do not "catch on," these struggling children become frustrated; confidence is lost, and they feel "dumb." In fact, most of these children simply lack a skill that can be taught to them: *phonemic awareness*!

A few years ago, children showed up on the first day of school and teachers would show them the letter "A" and instruct, "This letter says /a/ as in *apple*." Educators assumed something very critical to the process of reading. They assumed that children were able to conceptualize the individual sounds of their language and isolate individual sounds from the other sounds in a word. Educators have learned that many children—two out of five—are not able to do this when they enter first grade and many who continue to make

Trainer Presentation: 20 min.

Lesson Emphasis: Participants will learn what a phoneme is, what phonemic awareness is, and why it is an important skill to teach young readers.

1. Say:
   - What is the first sound in star? **/s/**
   - What is the last sound in trumpet? **/t/**
   - What is the middle sound in wave? **/ae/**
   - What word am I saying: /t/ /ae/ /b/ /l/? **table**
   - Tell me all of the sounds in paper. **/p/ /ae/ /p/ /r/**
2. Define *phoneme* and *phonemic awareness*:
   - ***Phoneme***: The smallest unit of speech; one of the set of sounds that we use to create the words we speak. Includes consonant and vowels.
   - ***Phonemic awareness***: The awareness that our speech is made up of these separate sounds called phonemes.
3. Direct small groups to read the Discussion section together, or read it together as a group.
4. Summarize the content for the group.

Summary: Children with phonemic awareness are able to understand that the sounds of spoken language work together to make words. They can identify and manipulate the sounds in spoken words.

ParaReading
A Training Guide for Tutors

slow progress in reading persist with low levels of speech-sound awareness. Without this ability to identify sounds and to separate and blend speech sounds within their language, children have serious difficulty with decoding and, consequently, learning to read.

Phonemes are the basic building blocks of spoken language. They are the separate speech sounds that, when combined in seamless streams, create the language we so effortlessly use to communicate. The awareness that speech is composed of sounds that can be isolated from each other has proven to be one of the most fundamental skills for young readers to possess.

Tutors Know! *Phoneme*: a speech sound. Phonemic awareness allows one to identify the speech sounds in words. Examples: "There are three speech sounds in house—/h/ /ow/ /s/." "The last sound in book is /k/."

Your Turn to Learn

When you teach young children to read, it is important to be able to understand and sympathize with what they are experiencing. You are a reader. This makes it a challenge to understand students' experiences as they learn to read or work to improve their reading skills. It is critical to recognize that many of the students with whom you will work do not yet have a concept of the individual sounds, the *phonemes*, that make up the words that they read and speak. They have not yet developed phonemic awareness, and this may make learning to read difficult.

Your own phonemic awareness may not be as well developed as it needs to be to teach reading to young and struggling readers. Many adults need practice. This section will prepare you to include phoneme instruction in your lessons by building your *personal* understanding of phonemic awareness.

Tutors Know! When you see a letter inside of two marks, like /m/, you say the sound represented by the letter, not the letter name.

Trainer Presentation

Phonemic awareness is a linguistic skill, an oral language skill, and an awareness of spoken units.

Young readers who have phonemic awareness make sense of the letter-sound system and learn to decode, read, and spell more easily.

ParaReading
A Training Guide for Tutors

What Phonemic Awareness Is

Phonemes are the individual sounds that combine to create the language we speak. For example, the sounds /t/, /ă/, and /k/ are separate sounds that we create with our tongues, teeth, and throats, and they can be arranged in a certain order to create the word *cat*. There are 43 different phonemes in the English language. Every language has a unique set of phonemes.

The following chart presents the 43 phonemes and examples of the sounds in words. The phonemes are divided into consonant sounds and vowel sounds. Practice saying these sounds with your trainer. When you say the sounds, be very careful not to add an additional separate sound, /ŭ/, to these sounds. Say /b/, not /buh/. Notice these characteristics when you practice saying the sounds:

- Feel your throat as you say each consonant sound. Do you feel a vibration? Is the sound a "voiced" sound or an "unvoiced" sound? Be careful! You will discover that there are sounds you may be voicing when in fact they are voiceless!
- Use a mirror. What is your tongue doing when you say the sounds? Is it tapping somewhere in your mouth? Is it flattened? In the back of your mouth or in the front?
- Which sounds share similar articulation features?

Trainer Presentation

Transparency 6
Consonant and Vowel Sounds Chart

1. Present the vowel sounds next. Say all of the vowel sounds in order. Instruct participants to watch your jaw from the side as you say each sound. Discuss how the jaw drops and then comes back up.
2. Say each sound, and have participants repeat after you. Discover with them how the tongue moves from the front of your mouth to the back as you go through the sounds. *You may use* The Speech Sounds of English *video* (Moats, 2003) *to introduce the consonant and vowel sounds.*

ParaReading
A Training Guide for Tutors

Consonant Sounds			Vowel Sounds		
1.	/b/	butter	26.	/e/	see
2.	/p/	pet	27.	/ĭ/	sit
3.	/m/	mouse	28.	/a/	make
4.	/f/	fuzz	29.	/ĕ/	bed
5.	/v/	vest	30.	/ă/	cat
6.	/th/	think	31.	/i/	time
7.	/th/	them	32.	/ŏ/	fox
8.	/t/	tiger	33.	/ŭ/	cup
9.	/d/	desk	34.	/aw/	saw, call, water, bought
10.	/n/	nose	35.	/o/	vote
11.	/s/	smile	36.	/oo/	book
12.	/z/	zipper	37.	/u/	tube, moo
13.	/sh/	ship	38.	/ə/ (schwa)	about, lesson
14.	/zh/	measure	39.	/oi/	oil, boy
15.	/ch/	chair	40.	/ou/	out, cow
16.	/j/	judge	41.	/er/	her, fur, sir
17.	/k/	kite	42.	/ar/	car
18.	/g/	goat	43.	/or/	corn
19.	/ng/	sang			
20.	/y/	yellow			
21.	/wh/	whistle			
22.	/w/	wagon			
23.	/h/	hand			
24.	/l/	lion			
25.	/r/	rose			

Exercise #2: Practice saying these sounds with a partner and for your trainer.

Turn to the *LETRS* consonant and vowel articulation charts in the back of your workbook. Now, practice saying the sounds again using these charts as a reference.

Tricky sounds abound when we start isolating them from the whole words we speak. These are a few that you will need to know because you are sure to run into them with your students. What is the surprise in each of these?

Quilt = /k/ /w/ /i/ /l/ /t/

Box = /b/ /o/ /k/ /s/

Universe = /y/ /oo/ /n/ /ə/ /v/ /r/ /s/

Phonemic awareness is the awareness that our speech is made up of separate sounds. Phonemic awareness enables children to isolate the first sound, last sound, and middle sounds when they hear or say a word. It allows them to separate out all the phonemes in words and to match them to written symbols. *To think phonemically, is to consider the spoken sound separately from the letter we use to represent the sound in our written language.* This is difficult for adults who are readers! We automatically visualize letters in our minds when we hear speech sounds. Young readers must learn to match phoneme sequences to letter patterns. For many, the process of reading falls apart at the basic level of phonemic awareness.

Complete the Exercise: 15 min.

Direct the group to form pairs and practice saying the sounds to each other. Use this opportunity to move around the room and ask individuals to say the phonemes to you. Point to random sounds, ask for the potentially difficult ones: /zh/, the two sounds of /th/, /ng/, short vowel sounds and long vowel sounds. Note at this time any individuals who are having difficulty reproducing the sounds accurately. They may require extra tutoring and directed practice from you.

Lesson Extra: 5 min.
Participants become familiar with the more difficult sounds for *qu* and *x*, and the hidden sounds of *y*. Present these additional examples:

- **qu**: *quit, squash*
- **x**: *fox, axe*
- **/y//oo/:** *youth, unite, excuse*

Trainer Presentation

Transparency 7
LETRS Consonant Chart

Transparency 8
LETRS Vowel Chart

Direct participants to these charts in the back of their workbook. They can use the reference charts as they work with students.

Note: If the trainer is a LETRS trainer, the LETRS charts can be used to introduce the sounds.

Lesson Emphasis
Review and discuss phoneme and phonemic awareness. Examine phonemes in words to increase participants' exposure to and experience with phonemes.

Complete the Exercise: 10 min.

Ask the group to form pairs to review content up to this point through the key questions provided. Pairs share their written answers with the group.

Test and Practice: 30 min.

Lead the group through each of the phoneme tasks in this section. Teach the participants to understand the separate quality of the speech sounds by using visual aids, such as movable objects on the overhead projector, or by tapping fingers and thumb. Ask them to do it with you. Do not allow them to do these activities on their own yet.

ParaReading
A Training Guide for Tutors

Exercise #3: Review and Discuss

Turn to your partner, and ask and answer these questions: What is a phoneme? What is phonemic awareness? Why is phonemic awareness important for young children to have?

Work together to write your answers here.

Answers should show an understanding of these concepts: A phoneme is the smallest unit of sound that we combine to create the language we speak. Phoneme awareness is the awareness that our speech is made up of separate sounds. Children with phonemic awareness can isolate sounds in words and separate sounds from other sounds in spoken words.

18

ParaReading
A Training Guide for Tutors

Exercise #4: Test and Practice Your Phonemic Awareness

Do the following Phonemic Awareness Activities with your trainer.

Phoneme Matching

Read the first word in each line and isolate the sound that is represented by the underlined letter or letter cluster. Then select the word or words in the line that contain the same sound. Circle the words you select.

1.	**hook**	food	cloud	(foot)	(sugar)
2.	**laugh**	faun	train	sauce	(grand)
3.	**miss**	does	nose	(box)	(close)
4.	**cage**	(gym)	game	gnat	hang
5.	**think**	blunt	(sling)	(drink)	(hang)

Count the Phonemes

Count the number of phonemes in the following words:

through	3	loose	3	fox	4	knight	3
high	2	pitcher	4	judge	3	fir	2
pay	2	torch	3	strong	5	oil	2
wheat	3	quiet	5	vision	5	cream	4

Identification of Phonemes

Identify the third phoneme in the following words:

shoes	/z/	square	/w/	notched	/ch/
night	/t/	vision	/zh/	square	/w/
sing	/ng/	odor	/r/	walk	/k/

Trainer Presentation

Transparency 9
Phoneme Matching and Count the Phonemes

1. **Phoneme Matching**
   Say the first word. Ask, "What is the underlined sound?" Read each of the options in the row. Direct the participants to circle the words that have the same sound as the underlined sound. Repeat with the other rows.

2. **Count the Phonemes**
   Say each word then instruct the participants to put out one finger for each sound as you separate the phonemes together with the group. Direct the participants to count the phonemes with you. Model the correct segmentation of difficult items for the group then have them do it again with you.

Transparency 10
Identification of Phonemes and Segmenting Phonemes

3. **Identification of Phonemes**
   Say each word. Segment the sounds with the group by counting with your fingers from your outstretched palm. Record the third sound for each word.

Complete the Exercise: 30 min.

Materials—Chart paper or blank transparency

1. Group participants into pairs to complete the phoneme tasks independently. Instruct the pairs to stop after each task is completed. Review answers with them.
2. **Isolating Phonemes**
   Ask for responses from the group. Record their contributions on chart paper or transparency. List the words in columns under the key word. For example, under itch would be a list of other words with that sound.

(continued) **Exercise #4:** Test and Practice Your Phonemic Awareness

Now, pair up with someone and do the following phoneme tasks with your partner.

Isolating Phonemes—Think of three additional words that have the same sound as the underlined letter or letters in each word. List them. Be ready to share your collections of words!

itch	Examples: big, image, mi?
thought	Examples: mop, o? er, cough
tree	Examples: eat, receive, beet
boy	Examples: oil, toy, coin
bird	Examples: fur, under, dirt

Segmenting Phonemes—Segment and count the phonemes for each of the following words. Place a penny or other marker in each of the squares to represent each sound in the word. Record the number of sounds.

house	3	h	ow	s				
friend	5	f	r	e	n	d		
shelf	4	sh	e	l	f			
thought	3	th	o	t				
key	2	k	ee					
youth	3	y	oo	th				
fox	4	f	o	k	s			
knock	3	n	o	k				
scrunched	7	s	k	r	u	n	ch	t

(continued) **Exercise #4:** Test and Practice Your Phonemic Awareness

Note: The previous activity is commonly used to teach segmentation to young children. When teaching young children to segment, it is important to use one box for each sound in the words they segment.

Auditory Blending—Take turns with your partner and say the given word separated out into all of its individual sounds. Leave about one second between each sound and then ask your partner to identify the word. Do not look at the word if you are the partner who is listening!

Partner One: Separate the Sounds		Partner Two: Separate the Sounds	
Growth	/g/ /r/ /oe/ /th/	Swish	/s/ /w/ /i/ /sh/
Axe	/a/ /k/ /s/	Touch	/t/ /u/ /ch/
Swoop	/s/ /w/ /oo/ /p/	Phone	/f/ /oe/ /n/
Pitch	/p/ /i/ /ch/	Quick	/k/ /w/ /i/ /k/
Think	/th/ /i/ /ng/ /k/	Drum	/d/ /r/ /u/ /m/
Brook	/b/ /r/ /oo/ /k/	Chalk	/ch/ /o/ /k/

Trainer Presentation

Transparency 10
Identification of Phonemes and Segmenting Phoneme

3. Demonstrate with the transparency how participants will use moveable pieces to represent each sound in the words. When they are done, demonstrate the correct segmentation using the transparency. Ask them to do it with you.

4. **Auditory Blending**
   Ask for a volunteer. Role-play Partner One and Partner two. Demonstrate auditory blending with /s/ /k/ /oo/ /l/ = *school*. Monitor the group as they work through this exercise.

How to Teach Phonemic Awareness: 5 min.

Explain that *ParaReading* does not provide a reading program for paraeducators to use. The goal of the training is to establish conceptual understanding of the necessary underlying skills children need in order to learn to read and how to teach those skills. *ParaReading* was designed to increase the effectiveness of paraeducators' instruction with the reading programs that their schools already use.

Trainer Presentation: 10 min.

1. Explain that a child's awareness of sounds in words develops from a simple level to a complex level. The words we choose to use for instruction should reflect an appropriate level of difficulty.
2. Write the following word examples on a transparency and explain that there is a simple-to-complex word order that is important for them to be aware of. Show participants the differences in each word when compared to the previous word: *at, cat, scat, scant*
3. Explain that simple CV, VC, or CVC words are easiest to segment and blend.
    - Words with beginning and ending blends and words with vowel diphthongs are harder.
    - Define *vowel diphthong*: a vowel phoneme that has a mouth position movement when you say it—a sliding quality to the mouth position, /ow/, /oy/.
4. Say, "We do not want to use inappropriate words for our phonemic awareness lessons. We want to use words that match a child's level of phonemic awareness development."

How to Teach It: Phonemic Awareness

By including purposeful attention to phonemes when you tutor struggling readers, you are building a base that they will use to improve decoding and spelling. Prepare to include phonemic awareness in your lessons by using the advice in this section!

You will not do *all* of the following activities with your students in one lesson, but do spend about four minutes of your instructional time specifically on teaching phonemic awareness.

Choose Your Words Carefully

When you prepare to teach phonemic awareness, it is critical to consider and carefully choose the words you use. If your reading program provides lists of words for phoneme exercises, then you're set to go! If not, you will need to know how to match the words you choose with your students' phoneme ability level. Here are suggestions and examples of word choices that demonstrate an order of difficulty from simple to more complex.

1. Choose single-syllable words. The words provided by your school's reading program for reading practice are often the best to use for phonemic awareness activities too! Examples: *fan, pick, be.*
2. Use words beginning with continuant sounds for beginners. Examples /m/ and /s/.
3. If your student is beginning to isolate first and ending sounds, begin with words that have two or three sounds. For isolating middle sounds, make sure that your word choices are three-sound words. Examples: *cut, dirt, bead.*
4. Consonant digraphs (/th/, /sh/, etc.) represent one phoneme and are easily separated within words by early readers. Examples: *with, shot, chip.*
5. Avoid beginning- and ending-consonant blends until students can segment and blend words without blends. Then start with simple beginning two-sound blends. Examples: *blow, crutch, grace.* When students can segment beginning blends, use words with ending blends. Examples: *wind, milk, bent.*
6. Short and long vowel sounds are easier to segment than the vowel teams (/ā/ is easier than /ow/). Examples: *dot, doze* as opposed to *shout, foil.*

A Training Guide for Tutors
ParaReading

Exercise #5

Place these words in order of simple to complex using the headings provided. Provide another example word for each item.

waist flap at graft chief shift

fact night moist pup broil froze swift

2 or 3 Sounds	Initial Blends	Ending Blends	Initial and Ending Blends	Vowel Diphthongs

Multisensory Instruction

Multisensory instruction means that students simultaneously see, hear, and touch what they are learning. Teach your students the following multisensory cues to get them involved and to make it fun!

Multisensory Cues

- ***Tap the Sounds***—Beginning with your index finger, tap once for each sound as you move through each finger.
- ***Tap Head, Waist, Ankles***—To help students isolate middle sounds, use three-sound words and tap your head for the first sound, your waist for the middle sound, and then reach down to your feet for the last sound.
- ***Finger Count***—Count and say the sounds one at a time, raising a finger for each sound.

Complete the Exercise: 20 min.

1. Group participants in small groups of three and four. Direct the groups to categorize the given words by heading on the chart.

Transparency 11: **Choose Your Words**

2. Complete the table together after the groups complete it independently. Add words that were generated by the participants.

Lesson Emphasis: 20 min.
The meaning of multisensory instruction and examples of how to teach phonemic awareness with multisensory teaching.

1. Define multisensory instruction.
2. Demonstrate multisensory instruction using the cues. Use the following examples and words provided:
   - **Tap the Sounds**: *thorn, cork*
   - **Tap Head, Waist, Ankles**: *moose, booth*
   - **Finger Count**: *shave, throne*
   - **Pull the Sounds Out of Your Mouth**: *left, soft*
   - **Use Manipulatives**: *swim, pray*
3. Ask participants to discuss the complexity levels of the words used in the demonstration. Where would they fit on the previous chart? Which are two- and three-sound words? Which have beginning or ending blends?
4. Instruct small groups to practice these approaches with each other. Tell them to use the words in the preceding table.

Trainer Presentation

Lesson Emphasis: There is a continuum to follow when developing students' phonemic awareness. First we teach initial sounds, then ending sounds, and then middle sounds. Complete segmentation is next. Auditory blending can be a focus throughout.

1. Present each of the **Word Play** examples. Emphasize that this is play with a purpose.
2. Demonstrate how the multisensory cues can be applied during each of these using the examples provided under each heading. Instruct group to get up and do them with you!
   - **Isolate First Sounds**: *skin, gym* (Use manipulatives, move paper squares for the first sound.)
   - **Isolate Last Sounds**: *day, paid* (Tap sounds, then identify the last sound.)
   - **Isolate Middle Sounds**: *peach, touch* (Touch head, waist, feet—come back to waist, say sound.)
   - **Segment All Sounds**: *hand, pond* (Pull sounds out of mouth to show complete segmentation.)
   - **Auditory Blending ("Secret" Language)**: *plume, flute* (Do finger count; participants say word blended.)

- ***Pull the Sounds Out of Your Mouth***—Starting at your lips, pretend to grasp each isolated sound as you move your thumb and forefinger in a pulling movement away from your mouth.
- ***Use Manipulatives***—Little crackers, paper squares, or game pieces make good visuals that can help young children see the segmentation as they separate the sounds in words.

Word Play—A Developmental Continuum

When teaching phonemic awareness, engage the child in *word play*. Phonemic awareness is developed along a continuum. Children initially learn to isolate first sounds in words, then ending sounds, and so on. Practice each of these with your trainer using your multisensory cues.

- ***Isolate First Sounds***—Say the word and ask student to say the word and the first sound in that word. Repeat the word and sound with the student.

  Example: You say, "House." Student says, "House, /h/." Together, you say, "House, /h/."
- ***Isolate Last Sounds***—Say the word and ask the student to say the word and the last sound in that word. Repeat the word and the sound with the student.

  Example: You say, "Jump." Student says, "Jump, /p/." Together, you say, "Jump, /p/."
- ***Isolate Middle Sounds***—Say the word and ask the student to say the word and the middle sound in that word. Repeat the word and the sound with the student. Three-sound words work best.

  Example: You say, "Wave." Student says, "Wave, /ae/." Together, you say, "Wave, /ae/."
- ***Segment All Sounds in a Word***—Say a word and ask the student to tell you all of the little sounds in that word.

  Example: You say, "House." Student says, "House, /h/, /ou/, /s/." Together, you say, "House, /h/, /ou/, /s/."
- ***Auditory Blending ("Secret" Language)***—Say a word segmented into its isolated sounds, and ask the student to say the "secret word" back to you.

  Example: You say, "/l/ /ee/ /f/." Student says, "Leaf."

Tutors Know! *Complete Segmentation:* Separating all of the little sounds in a word—bead = /b//ee//d/. *Auditory Blending:* Blending the sounds of segmented word back into the whole word—/w//r//k/ = work!

Error Response

It is important to respond to students' errors in ways that will validate their efforts and draw attention to their errors as you correct them. Immediate feedback and correction will provide opportunities to increase learning.

1. Point out one thing that was done correctly. "Yes, the last sound is /t/."
2. Demonstrate the correct way. "Watch while I say all of the little sounds in the word: /m/ /ă/ /t/."
3. Point out the place where a correction was made. "There are two different sounds here, /m/ and /ă/, not one."
4. Student does it again with you. "Do it with me." If you're using sound markers, you and the student can pull down the sound markers together for each sound, saying the sounds as the markers are moved into the squares.

Data Recording

When you are teaching phonemic awareness, pay close attention to your students' responses. When errors are made, note what kinds of errors they are making:

- Are they able to do complete phoneme segmentation?
- Are they able to auditorially blend the phoneme-separated words that you give them?
- Are they confusing sounds? Example: saying /b/ for /p/, or /t/ for /d/.
- Do they consistently miss the last sounds or middle sounds in words?

Trainer Presentation: 10 min.

Lesson Emphasis: Participants learn processes for responding to student errors and recording student performance data.

Transparency 12
Error Response

1. Demonstrate Error Response: Ask a volunteer to come forward and to intentionally make an error on a task. Direct the volunteer to show all of the sounds in *mat* using manipulatives on the overhead. Volunteer makes an error, and you follow the process to demonstrate error response.
2. Repeat the process with a different volunteer, and use the word *punch* to segment all of the sounds.

Data Recording

Transparency 13
Phonemic Awareness Data Chart

1. Show what you would write for the first volunteer response, then work with the group to record data on the second volunteer response.
2. Tell participants that it is important to record student performance. This data can be used by tutors to develop appropriate instruction and to communicate about student progress.

Use the following box as a sample recording form.

Phonemic Awareness

Provide words when discussing errors.

1. Student does this well: (circle)

   initial ending middle segmentation blending

2. Student errors: (circle)

   initial ending middle segmentation blending

3. Sound confusion?

A specific notation about a student's performance will be very valuable feedback to the student's teacher. You will be an important asset to the reading program when you provide feedback that will help determine instruction for students.

Practice It: Phonemic Awareness

Exercise #6:

Use the following story from the *Read Well* reading program (Sprick, Howard, & Fidanque, 1999). Find 10 one-syllable words to practice phonemic awareness instruction. Then form pairs and role-play student and tutor with each other. Practice phonemic-awareness instruction using word play and each of the multisensory cues. When you are in the student role, make a few intentional errors to give your partner practice with error handling and data recording.

Choose 10 single-syllable words from the story and write them here. Order your words from simple to complex. For example, words with two sounds will come before words with three sounds, and these will be followed by words with initial blends and words having final blends.

1. Answers will vary: odd
2. it
3. see
4. town
5. then
6. from
7. sky
8. small
9. sound
10. clouds

Funny Weather Facts

One summer day, in a small English town, clouds began to darken the sky. People expected an afternoon shower. However, when the rain started to fall it was more than just a shower. The people could hear funny sounds. Whack! Plop, plop, plop! Plop, plop, whack! Everyone ran indoors. Then they started to see funny things in the rain.

"What is happening?" the people asked.

A little kid said, "I think it's raining cats and dogs." Everyone laughed. A man said, "Maybe the sky is falling!" Another man asked, "Do you think it could be something from another planet?" Just then, someone else shouted, "Wow! That rain is hopping, and it's green!"

The people shouted all together, "It's raining frogs!"

Do you think this story is fact or fiction? It is an odd story, but it is a real story.

Trainer Presentation: 30 min.

Lesson Emphasis: Participants experience the process of planning and teaching phonemic awareness.

Complete the Exercise

1. Read the directions with the group.
2. Instruct participants to work independently to choose their words for their phoneme lesson.

Transparency 14
Word-Play Exercises

3. Place **Transparency 14 – Word-Play Exercises** on the overhead for participants to reference while they prepare.
4. Instruct them to identify a multisensory cue for each of the five phoneme tasks and list them in the provided space on the next page.
5. Direct participants to form pairs. Each takes a turn as *tutor* and *student* to go through the five phoneme tasks (initial, final, and middle sounds, and blending and segmenting) using the multisensory cues they have chosen.
6. Instruct participants to practice error responses and recording data in their workbooks on the form provided on the next page.

Monitor the process as the participants go through the practice activity.

Provide positive feedback and correct and model with pairs of individuals to improve the instruction as needed.

Trainer Presentation: 10 min.

1. Praise the participants for their great work! Highlight specific examples of exceptional teaching from your observations.
2. Review a few of the potentially difficult areas that you noted during the practice exercise.
3. Direct participants to the Strategy Reference Cards in the Tutor's Tips section of their workbook. Explain that these can be assembled to make a quick reference for the teaching approaches learned in this chapter. There are other teaching ideas included in the Tutor's Tips, too!
4. Refer to the pictures that were posted around the room at the start of the training. "What would these individuals gain from what you know about phonemes? What would these students learn from you?"

ParaReading
A Training Guide for Tutors

(continued) **Exercise #6**

Use two of the words to practice teaching the following phonemic awareness tasks. List a multi-sensory cue you will use to teach each of the following skills. For example, you might select *Tap the Sounds* to isolate initial sounds.

- Isolate Initial Sounds ______________________
- Isolate Final Sounds ______________________
- Isolate Middle Vowel Sounds ______________________
- Complete Segmentation ______________________
- Auditory Blending ______________________

Error Response:

1. Point out one thing that was done correctly.
2. Demonstrate the correct way.
3. Point out the place where a correction was made. Explain.
4. Student does it again with you, together.

Data Record:

Phonemic Awareness

Provide words when discussing errors.

1. Student does this well: (circle)

   initial ending middle segmentation blending

2. Student errors: (circle)

   initial ending middle segmentation blending

3. Sound confusion?

28

ParaReading
A Training Guide for Tutors

Review: Phonemic Awareness

1. On what reading skill is Chapter 1 based? Phonemic Awareness

2. Why is this a critical skill? Children who have phonemic awareness learn to decode more easily. Children who do not have phonemic awareness struggle with the process of decoding and applying the sound system of our oral language to written language.

3. Where will you find words to use for teaching phonemic awareness? How will you know which are the best words to choose and use for phoneme awareness lessons? The words for the phoneme lessons will come from the reading material the children will be asked to read. If there are word lists used for teaching decoding, I will use those words. I will also choose one-syllable words without initial or final consonant blends until the student is segmenting and blending with words that do not have these.

4. Describe two procedures for teaching phonemic awareness. Any of the approaches practiced in this chapter: Tap the Sounds; Tap Head, Waist, Ankles; Finger Count; Pull the Sounds Out of Your Mouth; Use Manipulatives.

Trainer Presentation: 20 to 30 min.

1. Direct participants to independently complete the review.
2. Tell them that you will be coming around the room asking them to perform complete phoneme segmentation while they are working.

As the participants work, move around the room to assess question 6. Instruct the individuals to segment a minimum of three words from the words provided in question 6.

3. Gather assessment reviews, correct them, and record performance on the Assessment Record. Participants will want to see their assessments after you have corrected them. Make plans to return the assessments and allow for discussion.

ParaReading
A Training Guide for Tutors

(continued) **Review:** Phonemic Awareness

5. What do you do if your student makes an error?
   Point out one part that was done correctly.
   Demonstrate the correct way.
   Point out the place where a correction was made.
   Student does it again with me.

6. Be ready to demonstrate your ability to segment and blend phonemes with your trainer.

   Choose words from the following selection. Instruct participants to demonstrate complete phoneme segmentation. If participant is weak with this skill, indicate that the individual needs more practice on the assessment form.

crowd	quick	shirt
sleigh	throw	quiet
patch	sauce	boy
unite	throat	cage
mold	few	please
silk	jaw	box
show	crunch	pray
cheer	fruit	fax

ParaReading
A Training Guide for Tutors

Chapter 2: Phonics

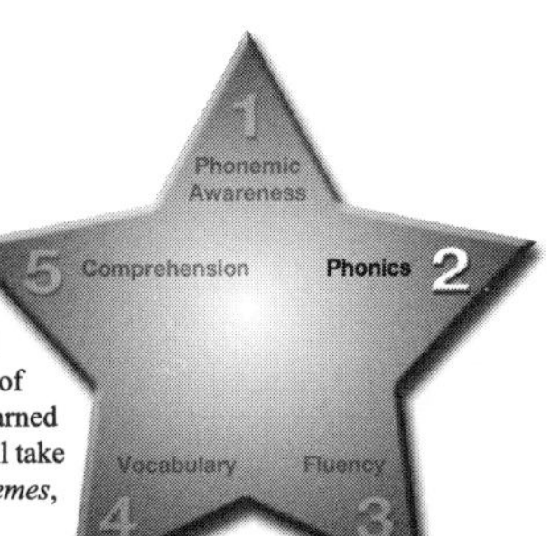

Discussion

A young or struggling reader faces tasks similar to those of a detective. Detectives decode mysteries, and readers decode words. Fortunately for readers, there is a consistent set of sounds that can be applied to letters and groups of letters to solve their mysteries. This application of sounds to letters to decode words is called *phonics*. We learned about *phonemic awareness* in the first chapter. Now we will take those same sounds and map them onto the letters, or *graphemes*, that are used to visually represent those sounds.

Studies have shown that the first strategy proficient readers apply when they come across an unfamiliar word is to sound it out. Studies that compare poor readers' brain activity with the brain activity of accomplished readers demonstrate how difficult this decoding process is for the struggling reader (Shaywitz, 2003). We also know that when students spend time analyzing words or decoding them, they are more likely to automatically recall that word the next time they come across it. Phonics, or decoding, is the application of analysis that originates from the basic structure of our written language.

Your school will most likely provide you with reading material that requires the teaching of phonics. The reading lessons may be direct and clearly outlined with a script to follow, or they may be vague, with little direction provided for phonics instruction. This wide possible range of instructional support requires that you be prepared and confident in your phonics skills and that you know how to apply basic instruction to help young readers improve decoding skills. Chapter 2 of *ParaReading* training will prepare you to use the instructional materials that are provided. Knowing the sounds of the letters and letter combinations and the ways to help students learn and recall those sounds are important skills for you to have.

31

Trainer Presentation: 5 min.

Lesson Emphasis: Phonics (decoding) is a critical skill. Children who become proficient decoders become proficient readers. Participants need to know how to teach decoding skills.

1. Define the difference between teaching *phonemic awareness* and teaching *phonics*. Say, "Phonemic awareness has to do with spoken language while phonics takes that spoken language and maps written language onto it." Simplistically, phonemes = sounds, while phonics = those sounds mapped onto letters. Phonics is graphemes and the sounds they represent.
2. Tell participants that no matter how well their school's comprehensive reading program is designed, they need to be comfortable with the decoding process and well versed in the basic teaching methods. This section will improve participants' own decoding skills and strengthen their ability to teach decoding skills to young children.

ParaReading
A Training Guide for Tutors

Your Turn to Learn

A good place to start when preparing to teach phonics skills is with a review of the individual sound-symbol relationships most common in our written language. As a tutor, you must:

- Demonstrate proficiency with the most common sound-symbol relationships.
- Use a multisensory teaching approach when decoding words.
- Work with instructional materials to teach phonics.

Phonemes are the *sounds* of our language; graphemes are the *written letters or groups of letters* that represent the phonemes. Phonemes are the spoken elements, and graphemes are the written symbols for phonemes. When we teach *phonemic awareness*, we ask students to provide *sounds*; when we teach *phonics*, we ask students to match *letters* to the sounds. Each is an aspect of language. Phonemic awareness is spoken language, but phonics requires the visual recognition of letters and letter patterns.

Tutors Know! Phonemes are the sounds, and Phonics adds the letters! *Phonemes* = oral language. *Phonics* = oral language plus letters!

With phonics, we teach children to match letters to sounds:

S h e l l → /Sh/ /e/ /l/

c h e e s e → /ch/ /ee/ /z/

Exercise #7: Phonemic Awareness or Phonics: Which One Is It?

Follow your trainer's directions to create phonics and phonemic awareness response cards for this activity. Listen to the sample teaching prompts. Determine if the students are being asked to use phonemic awareness or phonics, and hold up either the ***Phonemic Awareness*** or the ***Phonics*** card to show which focus skill is called for.

1.	How many sounds in *bat*?	Phonemic Awareness
2.	Sound out this written word: *rug*.	Phonics
3.	What silent letter is at the end of *game*?	Phonics
4.	What letter makes the sound "/s/"?	Phonics
5.	"/f/ /r/ /o/ /g/" What word?	Phonemic Awareness
6.	Spell the longest word you know.	Phonics
7.	Tell me the middle sound in *mom*.	Phonemic Awareness
8.	Tap the sounds in *lake*.	Phonemic Awareness
9.	Find another word that ends with an *-m*.	Phonics
10.	Say *bed* without "/b/."	Phonemic Awareness
11.	What two letters say "/sh/."	Phonics
12.	Spell the first syllable in *cracker*.	Phonics
13.	Change the /ŏ/ in cop to /ă/. What's the word?	Phonemic Awareness

Trainer Presentation: 10 min.

Lesson Emphasis: Participants discriminate between phonemic and phonic tasks.

Transparency 15
Grapheme-Phoneme Match

1. **Define Grapheme**: The letters and letter combinations that represent phonemes in our written language. Explain that phonics allows us to map graphemes onto the sounds in our language. Explain that there is not a one-to-one correspondence between *letters* and *sounds*. Show this using the transparency diagram.

Complete the Exercise

Materials—5" x 7" cards or half sheet of paper.

1. Tell participants to write ***Phonemic Awareness*** on one side of their response card and ***Phonics*** on the other side. Tell them to hold up the card to indicate which skill is being called for as you read through each of the tasks.
2. Explain the correct answers when there is disagreement in the responses. Ask, "Are we asking the student to apply letters (phonics) or only speech sounds (phonemic awareness)?"

Trainer Presentation: 20 min.

Lesson Emphasis: Participants will practice and strengthen their letter-sound correspondence. Trainer will informally assess participants' decoding abilities.

Complete the Exercise

Transparency 16
Grid One Empty

Transparency 17
Grid One Completed

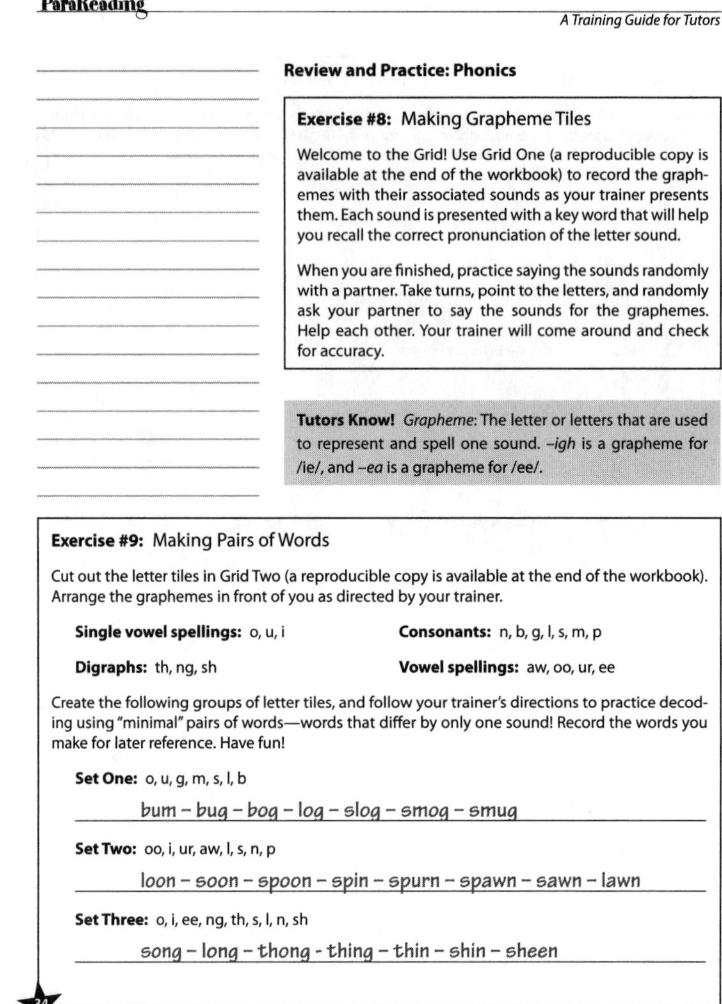
ParaReading
A Training Guide for Tutors

Review and Practice: Phonics

Exercise #8: Making Grapheme Tiles

Welcome to the Grid! Use Grid One (a reproducible copy is available at the end of the workbook) to record the graphemes with their associated sounds as your trainer presents them. Each sound is presented with a key word that will help you recall the correct pronunciation of the letter sound.

When you are finished, practice saying the sounds randomly with a partner. Take turns, point to the letters, and randomly ask your partner to say the sounds for the graphemes. Help each other. Your trainer will come around and check for accuracy.

Tutors Know! *Grapheme*: The letter or letters that are used to represent and spell one sound. *–igh* is a grapheme for /ie/, and *–ea* is a grapheme for /ee/.

Exercise #9: Making Pairs of Words

Cut out the letter tiles in Grid Two (a reproducible copy is available at the end of the workbook). Arrange the graphemes in front of you as directed by your trainer.

Single vowel spellings: o, u, i
Consonants: n, b, g, l, s, m, p
Digraphs: th, ng, sh
Vowel spellings: aw, oo, ur, ee

Create the following groups of letter tiles, and follow your trainer's directions to practice decoding using "minimal" pairs of words—words that differ by only one sound! Record the words you make for later reference. Have fun!

Set One: o, u, g, m, s, l, b
bum – bug – bog – log – slog – smog – smug

Set Two: oo, i, ur, aw, l, s, n, p
loon – soon – spoon – spin – spurn – spawn – sawn – lawn

Set Three: o, i, ee, ng, th, s, l, n, sh
song – long – thong - thing – thin – shin – sheen

34

1. Tell the group to write on their Grid One the letters that you will present on the transparency.
2. Say each letter and its sound. Ask participants to repeat each sound as they write it.

   Order of presentation: See completed Grid One for all key word associations.

   - The five short vowel spellings: a, *apple*; e, *echo*; i, *itch*; o, *octopus*; u, *up*.
   - The long vowels when the silent-e rule is used: a-e, *babe*; i-e, *hive*; o-e, *rose*; u-e, *tube*; e-e, *theme*.
   - Consonants: m, p, s, b, t, d, f, l, r, n, w, h, c (*cat*), c/s/ (*city*), k, j, g (*goat*), g/j/ (*gym*), y, v, z, qu, x.
   - Digraphs: sh, ch, th, <u>th</u>, tch, wh, ng.
   - Remaining vowel representations: ir, er, ur, ar, or, au, aw, ai, ay, ee, oa, oi, oy, ea, ou, ow, oo, ew, igh.

   Transparency 8
   ***LETRS* Vowel Chart**

   When the key word directs you to the vowel chart, show the transparency of the *LETRS* Vowel Chart and locate and show participants the alternative sounds for that spelling.
3. Instruct participants to practice with each other in pairs, pointing randomly to the letters and saying the sounds for those graphemes.

ParaReading
A Training Guide for Tutors

Grid One

35

Trainer Presentation: 20 min.

Note: Trainer directions for exercises on the previous page continue here.

Complete Grid Two Exercise—Making Pairs of Words

Transparency 18
Grid Two

Transparency 19
Tile Sets

1. Instruct participants to cut out the graphemes on Grid Two (creating individual "tiles") and arrange them in four rows as demonstrated on the Tile Sets transparency. There will be extra tiles; these can be set aside for later.
2. Instruct participants to say the sounds as they arrange them.
   - Single vowel spellings: **o**, **u**, **i**
   - Consonants: **n**, **b**, **g**, **l**, **s**, **m**, **p**
   - Digraphs: **th**, **ng**, **sh**
   - Vowel spellings: **aw**, **oo**, **ur**, **ee**
3. Explain that "minimal" pairs are words with spellings that differ by one sound/spelling. Demonstrate for the group as you take them through the decoding exercise with minimal pairs of words. Use transparency to perform the tasks by spelling the words in columns to model and correct.
4. Tell participants to group the grapheme tiles they will need as you begin each set. Tell them to spell the words you say using their moveable letters. Explain that they will change one letter each time a new word is given.

(continued)

5. Tell them to also write the words they make on the line provided under each set.
    - **Set One**: o, u, g, m, s, l, b
      Dictate each word:
      - bum
      - bug
      - bog
      - log
      - slog
      - smog
      - smug
    - **Set Two**: oo, i, ur, aw, l, s, n, p
      Dictate each word:
      - loon
      - soon
      - spoon
      - spin
      - spurn
      - spawn
      - sawn
      - lawn
    - **Set Three**: o, i, ee, ng, th, s, l, n, sh
      Dictate each word:
      - song
      - long
      - thong
      - thing
      - thin
      - shin
      - sheen

ParaReading
A Training Guide for Tutors

Grid Two

o	u	i	a			
n	b	g	l	s	m	p
th	ng	sh				
aw	oo	ur	ee			
f	t					
r	c					

Nonsense Words

When we want to check a student's ability to sound out words, to decode, we give them nonsense words. These are "make-believe" words that give us a sense of how well students are able to figure out unfamiliar *real* words when they come across them in their reading. Listen and follow along while your trainer decodes the following nonsense words.

vog	tel	ut
zek	zub	pef
trum	blesh	splin
gake	pune	lete
tark	yort	mir
soik	zail	shay
quawp	woam	prew

Exercise #10

Take turns with your partner and decode these same words. You will be asked to read a *new* set of nonsense words to your trainer during the review.

Trainer Presentation: 20 min.

Lesson Emphasis: We use nonsense words to assess how well our students can apply decoding to unknown words. It is important that participants can decode nonsense words accurately too! Teaching remedial phonics is a bottom-up process. Ask participants to read the first paragraph in the Nonsense Words section with you. Tell them that the ability to decode nonsense words helps us know how well unfamiliar real words will be decoded.

Transparency 20
Nonsense Words

1. Direct the group to follow along as you read the nonsense words on the transparency.

Complete the Exercise

2. Instruct participants to form pairs and practice reading these same nonsense words to each other.

(continued)

Transparency 21
Bottom-Up Process

1. Explain the bottom-up approach in explicit systematic phonics. Reference the diagram and tell them that our instruction begins with phonemes and builds to individual graphemes, then decoding words, then words in sentences and then connected text in paragraphs and stories.
2. Ask a volunteer to read the first paragraph of the How to Teach It section to further clarify this concept.
3. This is a good place to discuss systematic instruction. Ask tutors if they use a systematic lesson plan. Plan to show participants examples from programs. Ask participants to share their lesson plan formats.

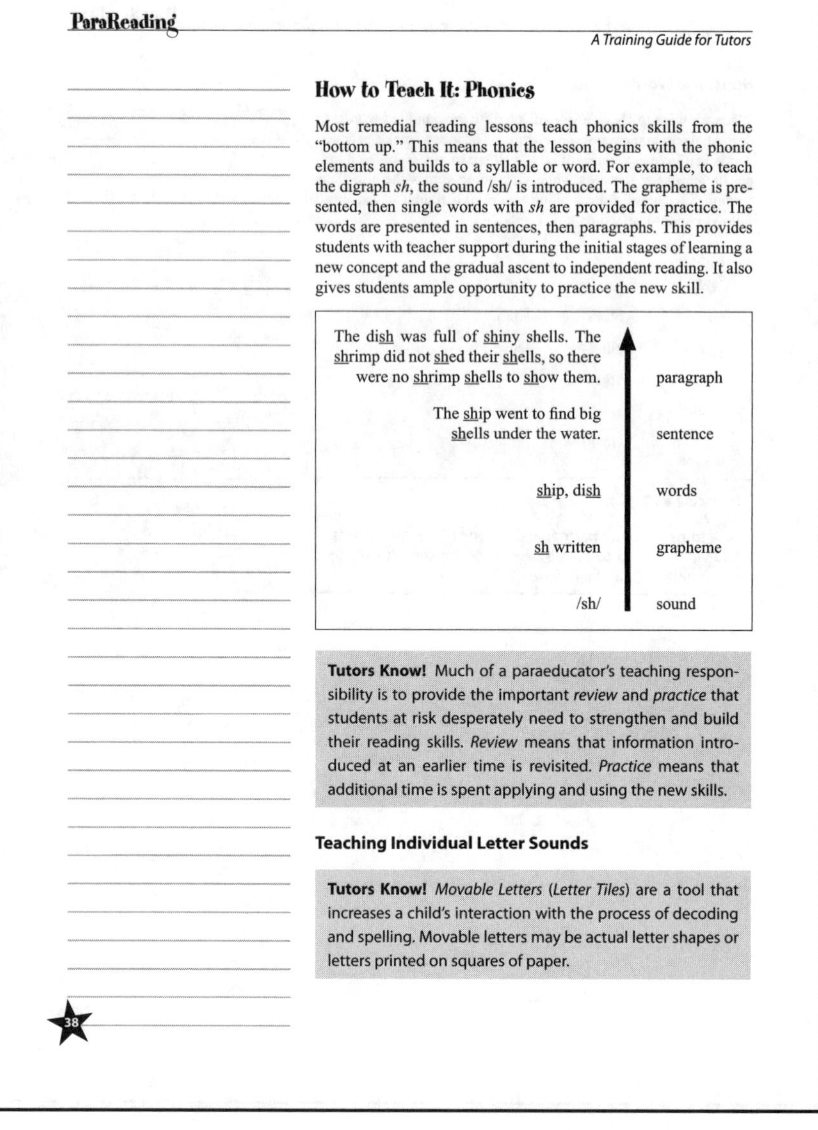

ParaReading
A Training Guide for Tutors

How to Teach It: Phonics

Most remedial reading lessons teach phonics skills from the "bottom up." This means that the lesson begins with the phonic elements and builds to a syllable or word. For example, to teach the digraph *sh*, the sound /sh/ is introduced. The grapheme is presented, then single words with *sh* are provided for practice. The words are presented in sentences, then paragraphs. This provides students with teacher support during the initial stages of learning a new concept and the gradual ascent to independent reading. It also gives students ample opportunity to practice the new skill.

Tutors Know! Much of a paraeducator's teaching responsibility is to provide the important *review* and *practice* that students at risk desperately need to strengthen and build their reading skills. *Review* means that information introduced at an earlier time is revisited. *Practice* means that additional time is spent applying and using the new skills.

Teaching Individual Letter Sounds

Tutors Know! *Movable Letters* (*Letter Tiles*) are a tool that increases a child's interaction with the process of decoding and spelling. Movable letters may be actual letter shapes or letters printed on squares of paper.

38

Before the strategies for teaching decoding *words* are introduced, it is important to discuss the student who is at the very early stages of decoding and just learning the *sounds* for individual letters. This student will require drill and practice to begin connecting the sounds to letters before blending them into words. To assist with this process, the teacher presents the letters and provides the sounds that are associated with the letters. Moveable letters provide a great tool for teaching the early stages of decoding.

Exercise #11
Find the following graphemes that you cut from Grid Two:

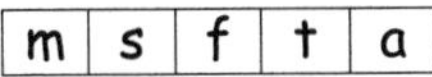

m	s	f	t	a

Role-play with your trainer. You will be the student, and your trainer will be the tutor. Follow the directions with your moveable letters to experience how to teach letter sounds.

Procedure for Teaching Letter Sounds:

1. "This letter *m* makes the sound /m/. Say it with me, /m/. What sound does the *m* (pointing) make?" "When we see *m* in a word, we say /m/."

   Follow the same process for each letter, teaching the sounds.
2. Point randomly to the letters, asking for the sounds. Point and say, "What sound?" Keep a quick pace. Make it lively: "I am going to try to trick you…"
3. Ask the student to show you a given sound. "Show me the /s/. Show me the /ă/."

Exercise #12
Pair up and role-play student and tutor. Use the following grapheme tiles:

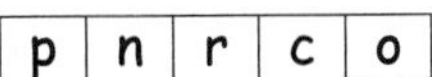

p	n	r	c	o

Practice the previous steps for introducing and practicing the individual letter sounds.

Teach the letter sounds and then ask two types of questions to provide extra practice:

- "Show me the /_ / sound."
- Pointing to a letter: "What sound is this?"

Trainer Presentation: 15 min.

Lesson Emphasis: Participants will learn procedures for teaching decoding and blending.

1. Tell participants that early decoding begins at the individual letter/sound level.

Complete the Exercise

Materials—Use letter tiles cut out earlier from Grid 2.

2. Instruct participants to find these graphemes from the letters they cut out in the previous exercise: m, s, f, t, a. Arrange your transparency letter tiles on the overhead.
3. Demonstrate steps 1–3, outlined in the text, to teach individual letter sounds.
4. Define the two types of questions. Student identifies: "Show me the /s/." Student produces: "What sound (teacher points to a letter)?"
5. Ask participants to form pairs and role-play tutor and student. Instruct them to use the letters: p, n, r, c, o. Direct them to use the script in their text to teach the letter sounds and then to ask the two types of questions. Monitor the procedure, and assist if needed.
6. Tell participants that they will now learn four procedures that can be used to teach *blending skills*. Read each of the four and then move on to define each:
   - Whole-Word Blending
   - Stretch-and-Say Blending
   - Tap and Blend
   - Sounds to Spelling

Trainer Presentation: 15 min.

Lesson Emphasis: Participants will learn procedures for teaching blending.

Transparency 22
Whole-Word Blending

Transparency 23
Stretch-and-Say Blending

Transparency 24
Tap and Blend

1. Read through the steps for each procedure.
2. Demonstrate each procedure after reading the description.
3. Write the words listed below on the overhead and use them to demonstrate for the group. Role-play this process with the group acting as students.
   - **Whole-Word Blending**: Demonstrate with *sand, fox, bath*.
   - **Stretch-and-Say Blending**: Demonstrate with *hug, flash, fern*.
   - **Tap and Blend**: Demonstrate with *cloud, quick, flop*.

(continued)

ParaReading
A Training Guide for Tutors

Procedures For Teaching Blending

This section outlines four procedures that you can use to teach decoding and blending skills:

1. Whole-Word Blending
2. Stretch-and-Say Blending
3. Tap and Blend
4. Sounds to Spelling—This method uses the *encoding* or spelling process as a way of practicing and recalling the graphemes that are used to represent sounds.

Whole-Word Blending

Another name for this procedure is "touch and say." Children touch each letter (or grapheme), say the sounds, and then blend the sounds to read the word.

Step-by-step procedure for decoding *shack*:

1. Point to the digraph *sh* at the beginning of *shack*. Say "sound"; students say "/sh/."
2. Touch each successive grapheme, saying "sound" for each one, /sh/ /a/ /k/, as the children make the sound that each grapheme stands for. Then go back and blend the whole word smoothly, running your finger under the word, left to right, at the rate of about one phoneme each half second.

   Continuous sounds are easier to begin with. For example, *bat* (/b/ /a/ /t/) and *check* (/ch/ /e/ /ck/) are a little harder than *shell*, *thin*, or *moss*.
3. Slowly compress the extended word. Go from *shshshaaack* to *shshaack* to *shack*.
4. Point to the word and say, "The word is *shack*."
5. Check for understanding of the word and the ability to use it in a sentence.

Role-play Whole-Word Blending with your trainer.

ParaReading
A Training Guide for Tutors

Stretch-and-Say Blending

Phonemes are segmented and counted and then the whole word is blended with an accompanying gesture to pull the sounds together into the word.

Step-by-step procedure for decoding *sun*:

1. Say the whole word, "Sun."
2. Ask students to hold up one finger for each sound they hear as the word is segmented and the phonemes counted.
3. Say the whole word while pulling your arm down or sweeping it across your body from left to right.

Role-play Stretch-and-Say Blending with your trainer.

Tap and Blend

This method is similar to Whole-Word Blending except that the student is actively involved with the decoding process through *tapping* the sounds as tutor and student work through the word together.

Step-by-step procedure for decoding *stick*:

In unison, tutor and student tap index finger and thumb together as they say each sound in the word and blend the sounds together. If needed, the tutor can touch each grapheme as the student taps the sounds.

1. Tap and say "/s/."
2. Tap and say "/t/."
3. Tap and say "/i/."
4. Tap and say "/k/."
5. Run finger under whole word and say, "Stick."

Tap and Blend adds a multisensory element that assists the student with connecting the individual sounds with the letters in words. As with any decoding method, children progress from oral decoding of words to silent decoding. Some students need more time to decode orally before transitioning to silent decoding and then to automatic decoding of unfamiliar words.

Role-play Tap and Blend with your trainer.

Trainer Presentation: 10 min.

Transparency 25
Sounds to Spelling Step-by-Step Procedure

Transparency 26
Sounds to Spelling Form

1. Explain that Sounds to Spelling provides practice with phoneme segmentation, decoding, and spelling. Read step-by-step procedure to the participants.
2. Demonstrate this procedure. Use a transparency of the Sounds to Spelling Form. Participants use the form in their text to complete the role-play exercise with you. Use the following words on the form. Supply manipulatives/sound markers or have participants use coins.

Sounds to Spelling:
Demonstrate with *shop, sand, shirt*

(continued)

ParaReading
A Training Guide for Tutors

Sounds to Spelling—Phoneme Grapheme Mapping

This method adds another very closely related skill to the decoding process: encoding. The student separates the sounds in a word and applies the grapheme for those sounds. That is, the student *spells* the word.

You will need the following materials:

- Copies of the Sounds to Spelling form or a sheet of paper with boxes and lines.
- Moveable sound markers—paper squares or little crackers, some small items that the students can use to represent the separate phonemes.
- Carefully chosen words from the student's reading materials.

Step-by-step procedure for decoding *book*:

1. Tutor says, "Book."
2. Student repeats the word and moves markers into boxes for each separate sound, saying the sounds as the markers are touched and moved—"/b/ /ŏŏ/ /k/."
3. The tutor asks two types of questions about the sounds: "Show me the /k/," and then, pointing to the second sound marker, "What is this sound?" Student says, "/ŏŏ/." These two questions can be repeated for different sounds in the word so that the student is responding to questions about all of the represented sounds.
4. Once the questions have been asked, the student is instructed to push up the markers one at a time and write the graphemes for each sound in the spaces, saying the sounds as the letters are written.
5. The student then writes the entire word on the line.

Role-play Sounds to Spelling with your trainer. Use the Sounds to Spelling form; a reproducible copy is available at the end of the workbook.

Tutors Know! Decoding: given a *written* word, sounding it out to *read* it. **Encoding:** given a *spoken* word, sounding it out to *write* it!

ParaReading
A Training Guide for Tutors

Sounds to Spelling

Student: ______________________ Date: ______________

____

____

____

Trainer Presentation: 20 min.

Lesson Emphasis: Participants practice and improve their use of decoding and blending procedures. They practice error response and data recording.

ParaReading
A Training Guide for Tutors

Practice It: Phonics

The use of moveable letters to teach letter-sound correspondence and four instructional strategies for decoding whole words were introduced in the previous section. Now it is time for you to practice using these strategies to begin building confidence and automaticity with their use. Additional practice with children is recommended. The following role-playing activities are designed to provide experience with each of the four strategies. Practice the Error Response procedure when the "student" makes errors. Record data as instructed on the data form provided.

Error Response

1. Point out one part that was done correctly. "This first sound is /s/; you were right!"
2. Demonstrate the correct way. "Watch and listen while I do it." Decode each sound correctly, and blend the sounds to say the word.
3. Point out the place where a correction was made. "This middle sound here (pointing) is /ŏ/; I heard you say /ŭ/. What sound will you say next time?"
4. Student does it again with you. "Do it correctly with me."

Exercise #13: Individual Letter Sounds

Pair up and take turns as student and tutor to role-play the steps for introducing and practicing individual letter sounds. When you role-play the student, make a few errors to give your partner practice with the error-response process.

- Tutor #1 uses the following letter squares: p, n, r, c, o.
- Tutor #2 uses the following letter squares: d, h, k, l, i.

Directions:

1. "This letter *m* makes the sound /m/. Say it with me, /m/. What sound does the *m* (pointing) make?" "When we see *m* in a word, we say /m/."

   Follow the same process for each letter, teaching the sounds.
2. Point randomly to the letters, asking for the sounds. Point and say, "What sound?" Keep a quick pace. Make it lively: "I am going to try to trick you...."
3. Ask the student to show you a given sound. "Show me the /s/. Show me the /ă/."

Data Recording

Provide recording data during your role-playing practice.

1. Student does this well:
2. Student errors:
3. Sound confusion?

Transparency 27
Decoding Data Form

1. Ask a volunteer to come forward. Use transparency letters p, n, r, c, and o to review the Individual Letter Sounds process with the volunteer. Ask the volunteer to make an intentional error.
2. Ask participants to follow the Error Response directions as you respond to the volunteer's error. Explain that this is the same response process that they practiced with phonemic awareness instruction.
3. Use transparency to show participants how to record responses.
4. Instruct participants to form pairs and follow the directions given in the text to practice teaching Individual Letter Sounds.
5. Monitor their teaching and use of the data recording form. Assist when necessary.

Trainer Presentation: 20 min.

1. Instruct participants to form new pairs and role-play student and teacher to practice Whole-Word Blending, error response, and data recording.
2. Provide 3" x 5" cards or self-stick notes. Instruct participants to write their words on cards to use for practice.
3. Instruct participants to form new pairs again and role-play student and teacher to practice Stretch-and-Say Blending, error response, and data recording.

   Monitor the groups and assist when necessary. Look for examples of appropriate use of the data recording form to show the groups.
4. Show a few examples of the data recordings from the groups that reflect appropriate use. Explain how the participants recorded helpful information on the student's performance.

(continued)

Exercise #14: Whole-Word Blending

Pair up and practice the steps for Whole-Word Blending. When you role-play the student, make a few errors to give your partner practice with the error-response process.

Please note that /ar/, /ou/, and /ee/ stand for single vowel sounds.

- Tutor #1 uses the following words: *crash, swim, steep.*
- Tutor #2 uses the following words: *brush, star, trout.*

Example—Whole-Word Blending

Step-by-step procedure for decoding *shack*:

1. Point to the digraph *sh* and say "Sound"; students say "/sh/."
2. Point to the *a* and say "Sound"; students say "/ă/."
3. Point to the *ck* and say "Sound"; students say "/k/."
4. Slide fingers under the whole word to blend it; students say "Shack."
5. Point to the word and say, "The word is *shack*."
6. Check for understanding and the ability to use the word in a sentence.

Data Recording

Provide words when discussing errors.

1. Student does this well:
2. Student errors:
3. Sound confusion?

ParaReading
A Training Guide for Tutors

Exercise #15: Stretch-and-Say Blending

Pair up and role-play the steps for introducing and practicing Stretch-and-Say Blending. When you role-play the student, make a few errors to give your partner practice with the error-response process.

- Tutor #1 uses the following words: *pine, tape, glue.*
- Tutor #2 uses the following words: *game, home, bike.*

Example—Stretch-and-Say Blending

Step-by-step procedure for decoding *sun*:

1 Say the whole word, "Sun."

2 Ask students to hold up one finger for each sound they hear as the word is segmented and the phonemes counted.

3 Say the whole word while pulling your arm down or sweeping it across your body from left to right.

Data Recording

Provide words when discussing errors.

1. Student does this well:

2. Student errors:

3. Sound confusion?

Trainer Presentation: 10 min.

1. Instruct participants to form new pairs and follow the directions to role-play Tap and Blend, respond to errors, and record data.

   Monitor the groups and assist when necessary. Look for examples of appropriate use of the data recording form to show the groups.

2. Show a few examples of the data recordings from the groups that reflect appropriate use. Explain how the participants recorded helpful information on the student's performance. Ask for comments on the processes that they just practiced.

ParaReading
A Training Guide for Tutors

Exercise #16: Tap and Blend

Pair up and role-play the steps for introducing and practicing Tap and Blend. When you role-play the student, make a few errors to give your partner practice with the error-response process.

- Tutor #1 uses the following words: *lunch, harsh, turn.*
- Tutor #2 uses the following words: *tooth, clay, boots.*

Example—Tap and Blend

Step-by-step procedure for decoding *stick*:

In unison, the teacher and student tap index finger and thumb together as they say each sound in the word and blend the sounds together. If needed, the teacher can touch each grapheme as the student taps the sounds.

1. Tap and say "/s/."
2. Tap and say "/t/."
3. Tap and say "/ĭ/."
4. Tap and say "/k/."
5. Run finger under whole word and say, "Stick."

Data Recording

Provide words when discussing errors.

1. Student does this well:

2. Student errors:

3. Sound confusion?

ParaReading
A Training Guide for Tutors

Exercise #17: Sounds to Spelling

Pair up and role-play the steps for practicing Sounds to Spelling using the Sounds to Spelling form. When you role-play the student, make a few errors to give your partner practice with the error-response process.

- Tutor #1 uses the following words: *bricks, farming, paint.*
- Tutor #2 uses the following words: *white, thirsty, healing.*

Example—Sounds to Spelling

Step-by-step procedure for decoding *book*:

1. Tutor says, "Book."
2. Student repeats the word and moves markers into the spaces for each separate sound, saying the sounds as the markers are touched and moved—"/b/ /ŏŏ/ /k/."
3. The tutor asks two types of questions about the sounds: "Show me the /k/," and then, pointing to the second sound marker, "What is this sound?" Student says, "/ŏŏ/." These two questions can be repeated for different sounds in the word so that the student is responding to questions about all of the represented sounds.
4. Once the questions have been asked, the student is instructed to push up the markers one at a time and write the graphemes for each sound in the spaces, saying the sounds as the letters are written.
5. The student then writes the entire word on the line.

Data Recording

Provide words when discussing errors.

1. Student does this well:

2. Student errors:

3. Sound confusion?

49

Trainer Presentation: 10 min.

1. Instruct participants to form new pairs and follow the directions to role-play Sounds to Spelling. Use the Sounds to Spelling form.

   Monitor the groups and assist when necessary. Look for examples of appropriate use of the data recording form to show the groups.

2. Show a few examples of the data recordings from the groups that reflect appropriate use. Explain how the participants recorded helpful information on the student's performance. Ask for comments on the processes that they just practiced.

Prepare Participants for the Review
(Plan about 30 minutes for the review process)

Instruct participants to form small groups and go back through the text in this chapter to review teaching processes, responding to errors, and recording data on student performance. Explain that you will ask them to read a few nonsense words.

Trainer Presentation: 20 to 30 min.

1. Direct participants to independently complete the review.
2. As participants are completing the review, ask each participant to read the nonsense words to you. Depending on time, have them read all or a selection of them to you.
3. Gather review assessments, correct them, and record performance on the Assessment Record. Participants will want to see their assessments after you have corrected them. Make plans to return the assessments and allow for discussion.

ParaReading
A Training Guide for Tutors

Review: Phonics

1. What skill is practiced in Chapter 2? *Phonics, or Decoding.*
2. Name and describe two blending processes used to teach decoding in Chapter 2. *Any of the four processes can be used: Whole-Word Blending, Stretch-and-Say Blending, Tap and Blend, Sounds to Spelling. Descriptions should be complete and give a sense of understanding and ability to use.*
3. What is the benefit of recording a student's performance when decoding? *When the student's performance is recorded, I have something to share with the teachers. I can use the recorded data to plan my lessons, based on errors the student makes. Data recording can help me keep track of how well the students are doing and whether or not they are improving.*
4. Describe the steps for responding to student errors. *Point out one part that was done correctly. Demonstrate the correct way. Point out the place where a correction was made. Student does it again with me.*
5. Be ready to decode a selection of nonsense words for the trainer.

Trainer: Use these to assess.

vish	*v-i-sh*	lac	*l-a-k*
koz	*k-o-z*	dav	*d-a-v*
sath	*s-a-th*	chod	*ch-o-d*
jite	*j-ie-t*	sone	*s-oe-n*
derp	*d-r-p*	nurx	*n-r-k-s*
groy	*g-r-oy*	meab	*m-ee-b*
faul	*f-aw-l*	digh	*d-ie*

Chapter 3: Fluency

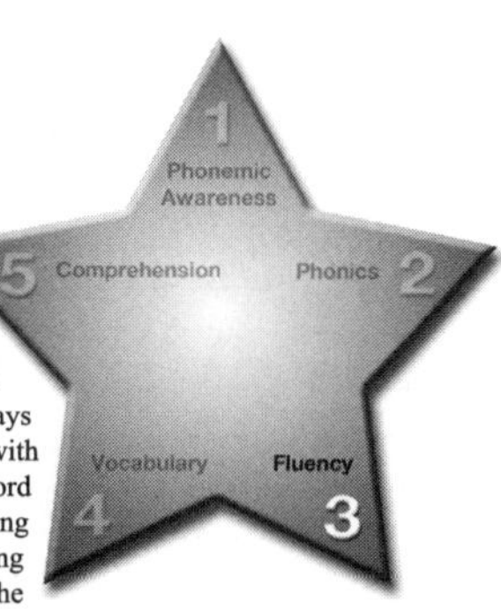

Discussion

The ultimate goal of reading instruction is for students to be automatic with the skills they use to read. Just like learning to play a musical instrument or ride a bicycle, there are underlying reading skills that, with practice and time, reach a level of ease that allows the process to happen effortlessly. Reaching this level of fluency isn't always easy. When students read fluently, they have automaticity with other reading skills: phonemic awareness, decoding, and word recognition. When a student is a fluent reader, the demanding tasks of decoding are automatic, and energy expended during the reading process can be directed to comprehension of the material that is being read. This is the ultimate goal for our students: to become fluent readers able to gain meaning from the written word, apply higher-order thinking skills, infer meaning, and expand their knowledge of the world from reading.

The first two chapters in *ParaReading* taught us about phonemic awareness through sound segmentation and blending, and applying letters to sounds through phonics and spelling. Chapter 3 builds on this instruction and focuses on working with students to build *automaticity* with these skills so that students can develop fluent reading habits. Previous studies have shown that trained tutors play an important role with helping young readers to significantly improve reading fluency (Glaser, 2002).

What does it mean to read fluently? What does a person sound like when they read fluently? What can fluent readers do that non-fluent readers are unable to do? These questions will be answered in this chapter.

Your Turn to Learn

Listen to your trainer simulate two different students reading. Answer these questions:

- What does a fluent reader sound like?
- What does a disfluent reader sound like?
- What do you think are the advantages of being able to read fluently?

Trainer Presentation

Lesson Emphasis: Create an awareness of what fluent reading is, and why it is important to attend to fluency as part of our reading instruction.

Complete the Exercise: 10 min.

Materials—Use a child's text to demonstrate fluent and nonfluent reading.

1. Read aloud the first discussion paragraph. Define *fluency*: When a child is a fluent reader, the underlying processes (phonemic awareness and phonics/decoding) are automatic—reading appears effortless—and the child is able to direct energies toward comprehension of the text.
2. Instruct the participants to listen to you read. Read two brief selections from a children's text. Read the first example choppily and haltingly like a struggling reader. Read the second example smoothly and confidently. Read the questions in the text. Discuss.
3. Read the paragraph under the questions. Tell the participants that they will learn how to provide fluency training in this chapter.

Complete the Exercise: 5 min.

Transparency 28
Eye-Voice Span Passage for Fluency Exercise

1. Ask a volunteer to come to the overhead with you. Instruct the volunteer to cover the projection light at any time while you read the text aloud from the projected image. The rest of the class reads along silently *from the projected image* while you read.
2. Instruct the group to notice what happens when the text is removed while you are reading. Follow this procedure a couple more times. (You will be able to continue reading a few more words even though the projected image is removed.)

How do students become fluent readers? Many become fluent readers from lots of practice with reading, similar to the practice that is commonly prescribed to improve musical or athletic performance. Repeated skill practice improves the performance of a skill. To improve reading fluency for many students at risk, it takes reading practice plus additional *fluency training*. Fluency training is the instructional focus of Chapter 3. But first, let's look at the processes involved in the task of reading fluently.

Eye-Voice Span

Eye-voice span enables us to move our eyes ahead of our voice when we read. Your trainer will lead you through an activity that will provide you with an opportunity to experience eye-voice span.

What do you notice when the projected image is removed from sight? The trainer is able to continue reading a few words even after the image disappears! This ability is characteristic of fluent readers. When the reading process is automatic, our conscious attention is focused on meaning, and our eyes move ahead of our voice.

Helping students become fluent readers begins with teaching phonemic awareness and decoding skills. A firm grounding with these skills allows them to read isolated words and build automaticity with sight recognition. The frequent reading of connected text, sentences, and stories helps young students become fluent. Many students require special attention to reach levels of fluency that will allow them to progress with their reading skills. The common instructional process is to have the student read material several times until they attain fluency with the material. This practice is called *repeated readings*.

Repeated readings provide fluency training with:

- Letter decoding
- Single-word decoding
- Reading connected text

Repeated Readings

Fluency has been a focus of key reading research over the past several years. Reading fluency is measured by words read correctly per minute (WCPM) during the reading of instructional level material over three consecutive readings of the same material. The following activity has been prepared to provide an opportunity for you to experience the process and effects of repeated readings.

Exercise #18: Building Fluency with the Unfamiliar

Your trainer will take you through an exercise designed to help you experience improved fluency through the use of repeated readings. It is impossible for an adult to entirely duplicate the experience of a young child, but this practice comes close. During the process, pay attention to your responses, observations, and any questions that arise. Jot them down for discussion.

1. What were your initial reactions to the text?
   Participants may share that there were a lot of words to read, there were few recognizable words, they had to read slowly and haltingly, etc.

2. What are your observations with each successive reading?
   It gets easier, and there are words that are recognized and read automatically.

3. Did your initial responses to the text change with exposure through repeated readings? How?
   It got easier and began to look familiar. There was less stress!

Trainer Presentation

Lesson Emphasis: Participants will experience a simulation of the repeated readings process.

Complete the Exercise: 10 min.

Transparency 29
Automaticity: Repeated Readings Exercise

Transparency 30
Fluency Training: Repeated Readings Chart

1. Place Transparency 29 ***upside down*** on the overhead creating an unfamiliar and difficult image to read.
2. Ask a volunteer to read the material. (This needs to be a secure person who doesn't mind having difficulty in front of peers.) Time the volunteer for 15 seconds. (Tell participants to use one minute for actual repeated readings with students.)
3. Correct the volunteer's errors and hesitations. Use the repeated readings chart transparency to record numbers of words read correctly and errors.
4. Ask the volunteer about the experience: "How does it feel to read something unfamiliar, disfluently? What kinds of words are causing difficulty?" (The letters b, d, and p are usually tricky.)
5. Instruct the volunteer to reread the material again for 15 seconds.
6. Correct errors and hesitations after the 15 seconds. Again, record the numbers of words read correctly and errors
7. Compare the two readings. Ask the group for their observations.
8. End with a third 15-second reading. Discuss the experience and improvement.
9. Praise the volunteer for assisting with the activity.
10. Ask participants to write answers to the questions at the bottom of the page. Ask them to share their answers.

Trainer Presentation

Lesson Emphasis: Participants will learn the steps for doing fluency training through repeated readings.

Discuss the three levels of readers and the text that is indicated for fluency training:

- Letter Sounds—Train fluency with isolated letters; students say letter sounds.
- Words—Train fluency with isolated words; students say words.
- Connected Text—Train fluency with sentences and paragraphs; students read text.

Transparency 31
Repeated Readings Step-by-Step Process

Read the materials list with the group.

1. Read the Repeated Readings steps to the participants from the overhead. Instruct them to follow along in their text.
2. Use examples from the previous exercise to help explain the steps.

ParaReading
A Training Guide for Tutors

How to Teach It: Fluency

The steps for using **repeated readings** are outlined below and can be used with students from a variety of reading levels. Repeated readings can be used to build fluency with individual letter sounds, isolated words, and with reading passages.

Tutors Know! *Isolated words* means that words are presented alone, separate from connected or story text. A word list provides isolated words.

- If your students are just beginning to learn **letter sounds**, repeated readings are to be done with a page of letters from which letter sounds will be read.
- If your students are **decoding and blending single words** to practice building automaticity, do repeated readings with isolated words that reflect the target decoding skills.
- Once your students are reading **passages of text such as paragraphs and stories**, use these texts for repeated readings. This level of repeated reading generally begins around mid-first grade.

Materials You Will Need to Do the Repeated Readings:

- ***Reading material that is written at an instructional level for your student.*** This can be had in many ways: 1) Ask the classroom teacher to recommend appropriate reading material; 2) Use the classroom reading curriculum; 3) Use reading fluency training passages that are grade leveled and provide counted words for you.
- ***A copy of the page the student will be reading.*** You will use this to record student errors.
- ***A stopwatch.*** This is a necessary tool.
- ***Three colored markers or colored pencils to record the errors.*** Use one color for each reading to visually separate the errors in the first, second, and third readings.
- ***A copy of the Fluency Training: Repeated Readings Chart.*** A reproducible version is available at the end of the workbook.

Repeated Readings

Step-by-Step Process

Instruct the student: "Please read this passage for your fluency training today. Begin reading here (point), and read until I tell you to stop. If you come to a word you don't know, I will tell you the word." Time him for one minute, and note the number of words he reads. Subtract the errors for a total of words correct per minute (WCPM).

1. Chart the WCPM on the Fluency Training: Repeated Readings Chart. Show the student how to graph his own performance.
2. Review the errors with the student. Show and tell him the words you helped him with, words he omitted or substituted, and words he hesitated with.
3. Instruct the student to read the passage again, and follow the same procedure.
4. Do this for a total of three times, marking the errors with a different color each time. Have the student graph his performance after each reading. Work with the student to set goals between readings—"How many words can you read next time? Can you beat your time?"

> **Tutors Know!** *WCPM* means "words read correctly per minute." The total number of words that a student correctly reads in one minute is that student's WCPM.

Reading Errors

When you do repeated readings, you will also need to know what to count as a reading error. The following guidelines tell you what to count as a reading error:

- *Unknown word.* The student hesitates or attempts to read a word but does not produce the correct word in three seconds. Provide the correct word for the student and mark it as an error on your sheet.
- *Substitution.* The student misreads a word, substituting a different word for the actual word in the text.
- *Omission.* The student leaves a word out while reading.

Trainer Presentation

Read through each of the errors that are regarded as repeated readings errors.

Read through the bullets that identify what *not* to count as errors.

Ask participants to give you examples of each as you read through them.

Direct participants to review the error information with a partner prior to doing the following exercise.

Lesson Emphasis: Participants will practice the repeated readings process.

(continued)

ParaReading
A Training Guide for Tutors

Fluency Training: Repeated Readings Chart

Student Name: ______________________________

Words Read Correctly Per Minute	Date: ________ Reading Selection: ________			Date: ________ Reading Selection: ________			Date: ________ Reading Selection: ________			
120									120
100									100
90									90
80									80
70									70
60									60
50									50
40									40
30									30
20									20
10									10
0									0
	1	2	3	1	2	3	1	2	3	

56

Do not count as errors:

- Rereading words or phrases.
- Self-corrections made within three seconds.
- Skipping a line. (Do not count the words in the omitted line as errors.)

Exercise #19

There are several steps to follow when using repeated readings to improve reading fluency. Your trainer will now take you through each of the repeated readings steps with sample text. Review what to count as *reading errors* with a partner prior to going through the process, and then practice the process. Use the text and repeated readings chart provided.

Listen to your trainer read this passage three times. Follow along during the three separate readings, and note errors. Record the WCPM after each reading. Be ready to discuss your experiences.

Complete the Exercise: 15 min.

Transparency 32
All About Plants

Transparency 32a
Plants Article and Chart

Transparency 32b
Repeated Readings Chart, Single

Tell participants that you are going to be the student doing repeated readings. Their job is to listen, mark the errors on the passage in their book, and record them on the Repeated Readings Chart.

1. Ask for a volunteer to come up front. This needs to be a secure person because it is an unrehearsed task! Instruct this volunteer-tutor to provide words when you make three-second hesitations, to mark on a transparency (**32a**) the errors as you make them. Tell the volunteer to slash a word that is misread, slash a word if the volunteer provides it after a three-second wait, or slash a word if it is omitted. Show the volunteer how to do this. Tell the volunteer that the group will help! Instruct the group to follow along in their text and record errors too. They will use a different-colored pen for each reading.
2. Read the provided passage slowly, haltingly, with false starts like a poor second grade reader, for one minute. Between readings, ask the volunteer to correct your errors and any other words that were not fluent. The volunteer can take advice from the rest of the group for this.

Demonstrate after each reading how to record the information on the Repeated Readings Chart (**32b**).

Trainer Script: 45 min.

Trainer Script for All About Plants

Reading 1:

There are many plants on our *(hesitate 3 sec.)*. Plants can be big. Plants can be small. We can't every *(self-correct)* even see some plants. They are too small. Plants need many things to grow. They need sunlight. Some plants need a lot of sunlight. Others need *every* little sunlight. Plants need water to grow. Just like sunlight, some plants need a lot of water. Other plants need *every* little water. A *(hesitate 3 sec.)* can live without a lot of water.

Plants also] 4 errors / 74 WCPM

Reading 2:

There are many plants on our earth. Plants can be big. Plants can be small. We can't every *(self-correct)* even see some plants. They are too small. Plants need many things to grow. They need sunlight. Some plants need a lot of sunlight. Others need very little sunlight. Plants need water to grow. Just like sunlight, some plants need a lot of water. Other plants need very little water. A cactus can live without a lot of water.

Plants also need food from the *(ssss, 3 sec.)* to grow. Plants use *(omit)* roots to get food and water] 2 errors/ 93 WCPM

Reading 3:

There are many plants on our earth. Plants can be big. Plants can be small. We can't even see some plants. They are too small. Plants need many things to grow. They need sunlight. Some plants need a lot of sunlight. Others need very little sunlight. Plants need water to grow. Just like sunlight, some plants need a lot of water. Other plants need very little water. A cactus can live without a lot of water.

Plants also need food from the soil to grow. Plants use their roots to get food and water from the soil. The roots also hold up the plant. The leaves make food for the plant. They use the sun to make food. Stems are]

0 errors/ 121 WCPM

ParaReading
A Training Guide for Tutors

(continued) **Exercise #19**

All About Plants

0 There are many plants on our earth. Plants can be big. Plants can be
14 small. We can't even see some plants. They are too small. Plants need many
28 things to grow. They need sunlight. Some plants need a lot of sunlight.
41 Others need very little sunlight. Plants need water to grow. Just like
54 sunlight, some plants need a lot of water. Other plants need very little
67 water. A cactus can live without a lot of water.
77 Plants also need food from the soil to grow. Plants use their roots to
91 get food and water from the soil. The roots also hold up the plant. The
106 leaves make food for the plant. They use the sun to make food. Stems are
121 different on plants. The stems hold up the leaves and flowers on the plant. It
136 also carries water and food to the plant. The stem of a tree is hard and
152 strong. The stem of a flower can bend easily. Plants have seeds to grow new
167 plants. Some seeds are very small. Other seeds are in fruit that grows on the
182 plants. Some plants have flowers. Other plants do not have flowers. Plants
194 give us many things. They are good to us.
203

Words Read Correctly Per Minute			
100			
90			
80			
70			
60			
50			
40			
30			
20			
10			
0			
	1	2	3

Practice It: Fluency

Exercise #20

Form small groups of three or four. Use the sample repeated readings practice pages to practice repeated readings. There is one example for each of the three levels of beginning reader: letter sounds, isolated words, and connected text.

- Listen to the trainer simulate a child's timed performance.
- Record errors on the text as you listen.
- Record WCPM on the chart at the close of each minute's reading.
- Discuss, compare errors, analysis, and data recording with the other members of your group before the next reading.

Trainer Presentation: 45 min.

Lesson Emphasis: The repeated readings process is reviewed, rehearsed, and practiced.

Complete the Exercise

Materials—Use three different-colored pencils/markers and a stopwatch.

Transparency 33
Grapheme Sounds

Transparency 34
Isolated Words

Transparency 35
Connected Text (History of Flight)

1. Instruct participants to form groups of three or four. Give a participant the stopwatch, and ask this person to start and then stop you after one minute. Instruct groups to work independently to record the "student's" performance on the repeated readings as they listen. Instruct them to follow these steps for each reading:
   - Listen to you simulate a student's timed performance.
   - Record errors on the written text.
   - Record WCPM on the chart at the close of each minute's reading.
2. Direct a discussion following each reading. Project transparencies between readings with errors recorded. Instruct groups to compare errors, analysis, and data recording after each reading. More detailed presentation instructions for each level follow on the next three pages.

(continued)

Trainer Presentation

Read each of the following as scripted. Mark the errors on a transparency for the group to compare.

Make this last for about one minute. If letter is not in slash marks, say letter name:

Timing 1:

/ee/, /t/, /g/, one, /s/, /d/, h, /g/, w, /s/, /a/, don't know, h, /f/, x, /a/, /a/, /k/, /p/, /n/, /t/, /o/

- 10 correct/12 errors

Show your transparency with errors marked and total correct sounds per minute recorded on the chart. Ask a volunteer to come up and correct your errors.

Timing 2:

/i/, /th/, /g/, /l/, /s/, /d/, h, /g/, don't know, /s/, /a/, /u/, h, /f/, /x/, /i/, /a/, /k/, /p/, /n/, /t/, /o/, /v/, /m/, /p/, don't know, /s/, /y/

- 20 correct/8 errors

Show your transparency with errors marked and total correct sounds per minute recorded on the chart. Ask the same volunteer to come up and correct your errors.

Timing 3:

/i/, /th/, /g/, /l/, /s/, /b/,/h/, /g/, /w/, /s/, /a/, /u/,/h/, /f/, /x/, /e/, /a/, /ch/, /p/, /n/, /t/, /o/, /v/, /m/, /p/, don't know, /s/, /y/, /n/, /k/, /b/, /j/, /l/, /s/, /b/, /y/

- 31 correct/5 errors

Show your transparency with errors marked and total correct sounds per minute recorded on the chart. Ask the same volunteer to come up and correct your errors.

Ask participants to share their experiences with the whole group.

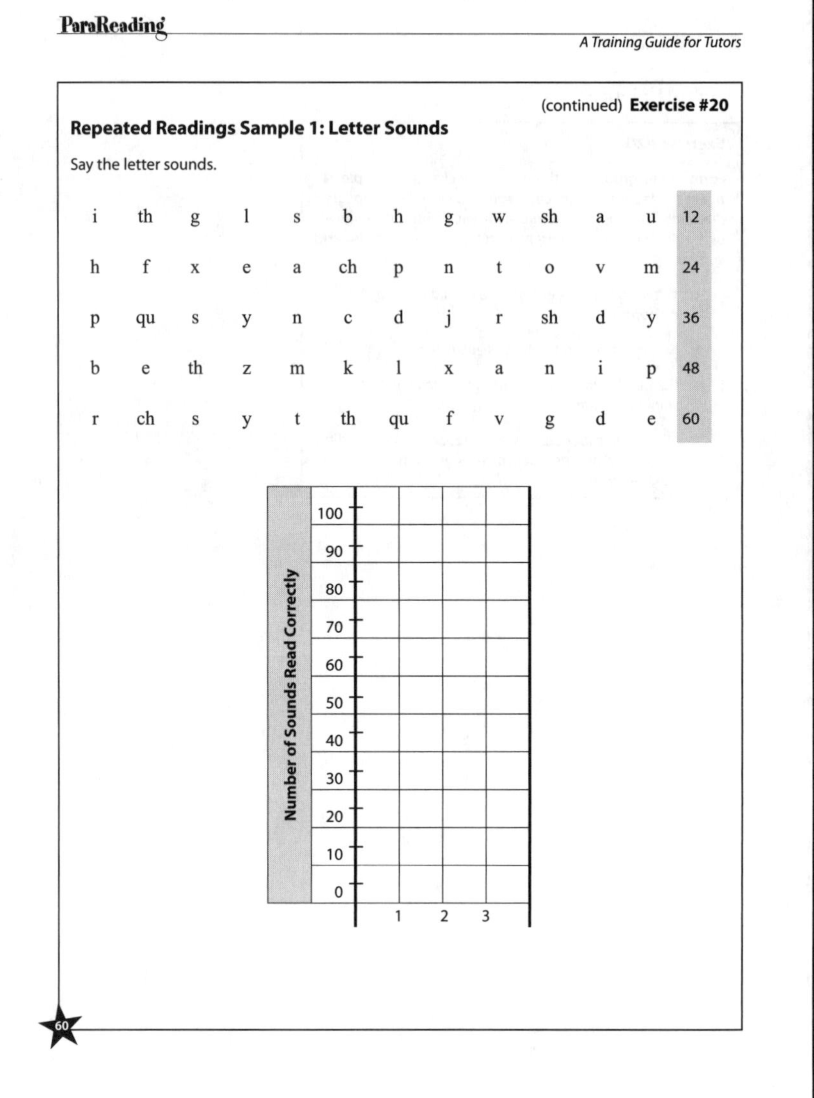
ParaReading
A Training Guide for Tutors

(continued) **Exercise #20**

Repeated Readings Sample 1: Letter Sounds

Say the letter sounds.

i	th	g	l	s	b	h	g	w	sh	a	u	12
h	f	x	e	a	ch	p	n	t	o	v	m	24
p	qu	s	y	n	c	d	j	r	sh	d	y	36
b	e	th	z	m	k	l	x	a	n	i	p	48
r	ch	s	y	t	th	qu	f	v	g	d	e	60

60

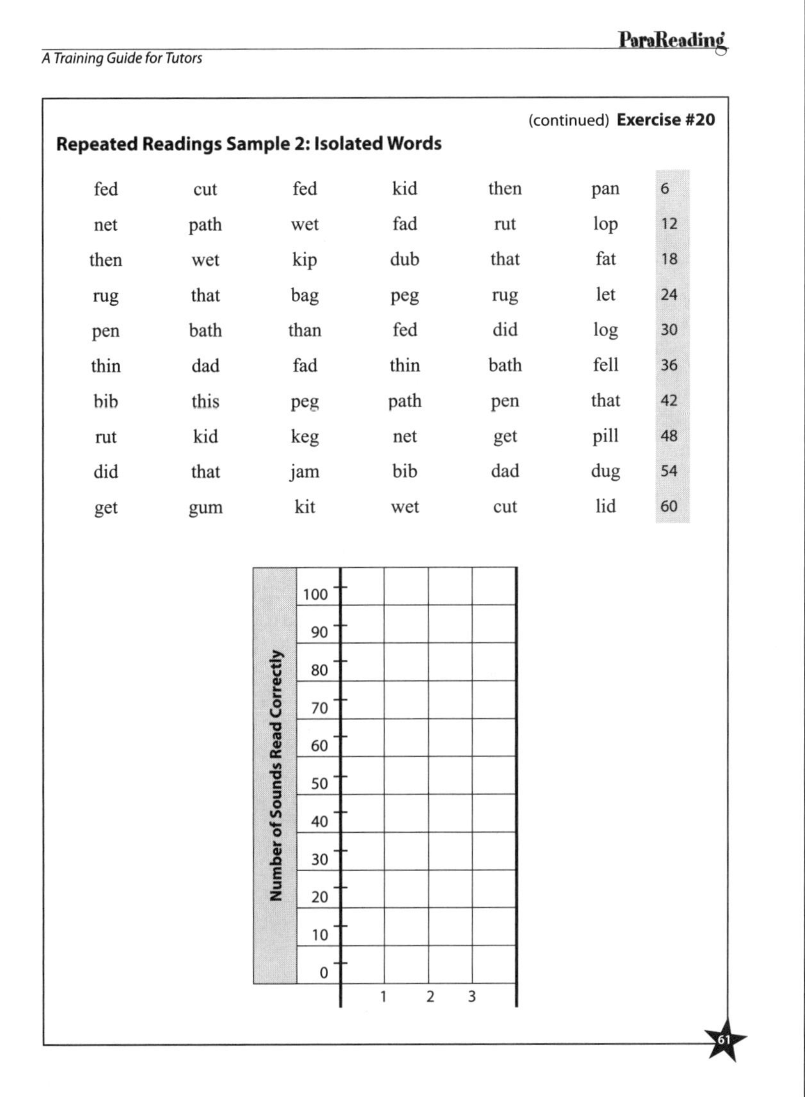
ParaReading
A Training Guide for Tutors

(continued) **Exercise #20**

Repeated Readings Sample 2: Isolated Words

fed	cut	fed	kid	then	pan	6
net	path	wet	fad	rut	lop	12
then	wet	kip	dub	that	fat	18
rug	that	bag	peg	rug	let	24
pen	bath	than	fed	did	log	30
thin	dad	fad	thin	bath	fell	36
bib	this	peg	path	pen	that	42
rut	kid	keg	net	get	pill	48
did	that	jam	bib	dad	dug	54
get	gum	kit	wet	cut	lid	60

Trainer Presentation

Read each of the following as scripted. Mark the errors on a transparency for the group to compare.

Give the stopwatch to another person in the group to direct you to start and then stop you after one minute.

Note: Reading across, make each set last about one minute.

Timing 1:

fed, cute, fed, kid, then, pan, net, path, wet, fade, root, lop, then, wet, kip, dub, that, fat, rug

- 16 correct/3 errors

Show your transparency with errors marked and total correct words per minute recorded on the chart. Ask a volunteer to come up and correct your errors.

Timing 2:

fed, cut, fed, kid, then, pan, net, path, wet, fad, rut, lop, then, wet, kip, dub, that, fat, rug, that, bag, pig, rug, let, pen, bath, then, feed, did,

- 26 correct/3 errors

Show your transparency with errors marked and total correct words per minute recorded on the chart. Ask the volunteer to come up and correct your errors.

Timing 3:

fed, cut, fed, kid, then, pan, net, path, wet, fad, rut, lop, then, wet, kip, dub, that, fat, rug, that, bag, peg, rug, let, pen, bath, than, fed, did, log, thin, dad, fad, thin, bath, fell, bib, this, peg, path, pen

- 41 correct/ 0 errors

Show your transparency with errors marked and total correct words per minute recorded on the chart. Ask the volunteer to come up and correct your errors.

Ask participants to share their experiences with the whole group.

Trainer Presentation

Read each of the following as scripted. Mark the errors on a transparency for the group to compare.

Ask for volunteer to be the tutor for you. Tell her that you will hesitate for more than three seconds on some words. The tutor should tell you the word, and then the word should be marked wrong.

1. For *[hesitate, sound out]* thousands of years, people *[try to sound out but miss it]* dreamed of *[hesitate for 3 seconds]* traveling in the air like birds. The only *[sound it out]* problem was, people had no way to fly. Then about two hundred years ago, two French brothers made a *large* balloon. They lit a small fire under the balloon and watched as the balloon rose in the air. Their balloon was flying!]
   - 54 WRCP/3 errors

Show transparency with errors marked and chart completed with words correct per minute. Ask for corrections.

2. For *[hesitate]* thousands of years, people *[sound it out]* dreamed of *[hesitate, sound it out]* traveling in the air like birds. The only problem was, people had no way to fly. Then about two hundred years ago, two French brothers made a big balloon. They lit a small fire under the balloon and watched as the balloon rose in the air. Their balloon was flying! Would you like to *[try to sound it out, miss it]* understand how the hot air balloon could fly? Hot air is *[I don't know]* lighter than cold]
   - 73 WRCM/2 errors

(continued) **Exercise #20**

A History of Flight: Hot Air Balloons

0 For thousands of years, people dreamed of traveling in the air like birds. The only
15 problem was, people had no way to fly. Then, about two hundred years ago, two French
31 brothers made a big balloon. They lit a small fire under the balloon and watched as the
49 balloon rose in the air. Their balloon was flying!
57 Would you like to understand how the hot air balloon could fly? Hot air is lighter
73 than cold air. When the brothers lit the fire, as the air got hotter, it got lighter, and the
92 balloon began to fly. What do you think happened when the air in the balloon got cold?
109 The brothers put a rooster, a sheep, and a duck on the first flight of their balloon.
126 Before long, many people rode in hot air balloons.
135

Number of Words Read Correctly
100
90
80
70
60
50
40
30
20
10
0
1 2 3

3. *[Read slowly but correctly from the main text. Finish with this line: ...*and the balloon began to fly. What do you think]
   - 99 WRCM/0 errors

Show transparency with chart recording total words correct. Ask for questions and experiences from the group.

Trainer Presentation: 15 min.

Ask participants to review this chapter in preparation for the Review assessment. Tell them that there will be a question asking them to review material in previous chapters. Give them about 15 minutes to review the material with their small groups.

ParaReading
A Training Guide for Tutors

Review: Fluency

1. Why is reading fluency a critical skill for students to improve?
   Children who are fluent readers are no longer glued to the decoding process. They have automatic access to the written word, therefore meaning and comprehension are more easily accessed. Fluent readers recognize when they can read fast (when the meaning is instantly available) and when they need to read slowly (when meaning is not as readily available).

2. What process do effective tutors use to help students improve reading fluency? Explain.
   Repeated readings. Students read a passage, written at their instructional level, three times. Each reading is timed for one minute. Words read correctly are counted and charted for each reading. Errors are pointed out and corrected between readings.

3. What will you count as errors during repeated readings?
   Words a student doesn't know or that are read incorrectly. Omitted words.

4. What does not constitute an error?
   Skipped lines. Self-corrections made within three seconds. Repeated words or phrases.

5. List, in order, the first three skills that have been introduced in *ParaReading* and an example of how to teach each skill
   Phonemic Awareness: any of the multisensory approaches; initial, middle, and ending sounds, and blending and segmentation.
   Phonics: Any of the four blending approaches; Whole-Word Blending, Stretch and Say, Tap and Blend, and Sounds to Spelling.
   Fluency: Repeated readings and a brief description of the process. All of the reading skills contribute to the development of a fluent reader. Repeated readings is a training approach that helps to build fluency.

63

Trainer Presentation: 20 to 30 min.

1. Direct participants to independently complete the review.
2. Gather assessments, correct them, and record performance on the Assessment Record. Participants will want to see their assessments after you have corrected them. Make plans to return the assessments and allow for discussion.

Chapter 4: Vocabulary

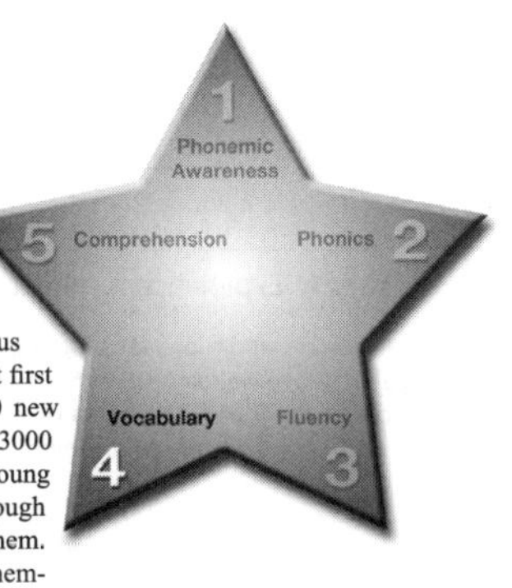

Discussion

What does it mean to *know* a word? How do people learn the *meanings* of words? Why is *vocabulary* an important reading skill? These questions have been asked and studied by reading researchers for many years. We have learned that knowing a word's meaning helps us recognize the word when we see it in print. We know that first and second grade children need to learn more than 800 new words per year and older children need to learn 2000 to 3000 new words a year to be considered effective readers. Young children learn a substantial number of these words through hearing when stories and informational text are read to them. Older children learn most new words through reading themselves (Biemiller, 1999; Nagy & Anderson, 1984).

Even though young children can and should learn word meanings through listening to text (both narrative stories and expository or informational texts), listening can only supplement and not replace critical reading practice for older children. These children need exposure to vocabulary through reading in order to build a visual reference of words for future reading fluency.

Yet, the reality is that many children come to school from environments where they receive limited exposure to language and therefore have fewer opportunities to build the vocabulary that would improve their reading comprehension. These kids are behind from the start, and it is critical that schools provide many opportunities for them to increase their vocabulary knowledge.

Phonemic awareness and phonics instruction prepare children to figure out new words when they are reading. Once those words are decoded, comprehension of the text is strengthened if the child *knows the meanings of the words*. There are four major processors that work together to help us read and comprehend what we read, as shown on the diagram on the next page. This model also provides us with a basis from which to evaluate and plan instruction for students. The *orthographic processor* is the first to receive input from the printed page. This visual information is combined with a word's phonological information to decode words. Once a word is decoded, the *meaning processor* matches it with a known word, and its meaning is accessed. If the word is unknown, then comprehension is jeopardized. It is important to know that once a word's meaning is stored in the word-meaning area of the brain,

Important: Prior to teaching this chapter, study the Four-Part Processing System section at the end of the lessons.

Trainer Presentation

Lesson Emphasis: All of the four processors are necessary for proficient reading to occur. Four processors help students bring meaning to written language.

Transparency 36a
Four-Part Processing System

Materials: *pictures and words cut from transparency film*

Copy the pictures, words, letters, and sounds on Transparency 36b and give to participants.

1. Read the Discussion with the group. Ask participants to turn to the four-part processing model.
2. Discuss each processor's contribution to reading.

Complete the Exercise: 20 min.

Instruct participants to cut out pictures and words.

"I am going to present a scenario where a child has a story read to him. At varying times throughout the scenario, I will ask you to consider which processors are being used. We will place the pictures or text on the different processors to illustrate their use. For example, which processors would be used when you read the word *book*?" Elicit responses. "Orthographic, because you accessed the *visual* sequence of letters to read the word. Phonological, because in order to read we connect letters with *sounds*. Meaning, because we have *book* stored as a *vocabulary* word. But not Context because we lack a *context* within which to interpret the word. Is it a *book* we read? Is it the process of being put in jail? *Book him, Danno!*"

(continued)

Read: "A child is listening to a story being read by his teacher. The written story is visible to the child in a big book format so that he can see the words as he hears them being spoken. As the child *listens*, he moves his gaze between text and pictures. The story is about clouds in the sky, and the child processes the oral word *clouds* as *clowns* and interprets this as *clowns in the sky*."

"Place the stimulus pictures on the model to demonstrate what you know about this child's processing at this point." Point to each of the processor circles and ask, "Is this processor being used? Explain." (No orthographic—the child is not reading the words. Phonological—confusion between /n/ and /d/. Meaning/Vocabulary—clown picture = funny man. Context—clowns in sky picture). Demonstrate for the group on overhead. Explain each processor's role for the student at this point.

Continue: "As the child listens to the story about the clowns moving across the sky, changing shape and color as the sun is setting, he has a difficult time matching what he knows about clowns and what he is hearing. He looks at the text, sees *clouds*, and reads *clouds*."

"Place stimulus pictures on the model to show this child's processing now!" Lead participants through each processor. Orthographic—letters for clouds, word clouds. Phonological—correct sounds for clouds. Meaning/Vocabulary—fluffy white shapes in the sky. Context—picture of fluffy white shapes in the sky.

Synthesize and summarize this exercise for the group. All processors work together to make efficient reading possible.

Additional: Create a "Big Book" with chart paper to enhance Exercise #21. Copy the following story. Place a large self-stick note with *clowns* written on it over the word *clouds*. Leave *clouds* exposed where bolded. Read this "Big Book" as you take participants through the exercise. Add a few pictures of clouds to further simulate the process.

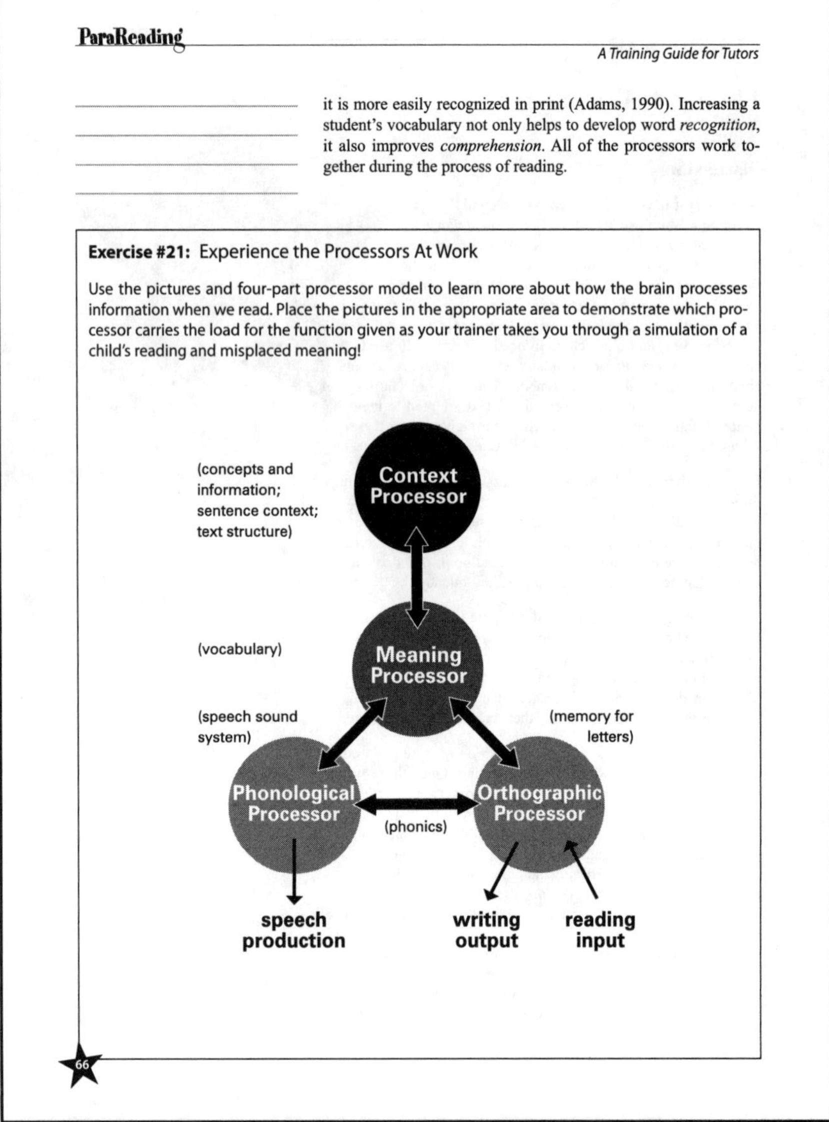
ParaReading
A Training Guide for Tutors

it is more easily recognized in print (Adams, 1990). Increasing a student's vocabulary not only helps to develop word *recognition*, it also improves *comprehension*. All of the processors work together during the process of reading.

Exercise #21: Experience the Processors At Work

Use the pictures and four-part processor model to learn more about how the brain processes information when we read. Place the pictures in the appropriate area to demonstrate which processor carries the load for the function given as your trainer takes you through a simulation of a child's reading and misplaced meaning!

66

Read the words *clouds* as *clouds,* but emphasize that the child hears *clowns*.

What do you see when you look up into the sky?

Sometimes we see stars twinkling in the darkness of night.

Sometimes we see stretches of blue as far and wide as an ocean.

Sometimes we see clouds (cover with *clowns*) in the sky.

Clouds (cover with *clowns*) float and change before our eyes.

They seem to play with each other, dancing across the blue stage. Clouds (cover with *clowns*) in the sky! (Discuss the child's processors activation here.)

When daytime is ending, clouds (*clowns*) in the sky change color: pinks, reds, and purples.
clouds

The sky is the artist's canvas. Clouds are the ever-changing pictures. Clouds in the sky.

ParaReading
A Training Guide for Tutors

Your Turn to Learn

In this next section, you will participate in several exercises designed to increase your awareness of vocabulary and to prepare you to pay attention to vocabulary in your work with children. Are you ready? Here we go!

Context, Morphemes, and Figurative Language

The English language is called a complex or "deep" language because it has several origins, which affect spelling and pronunciation and help us determine meanings of words. As a result of its hybrid nature, English is a rich language.

To determine the meanings of words, we use several approaches:

- We consider the *context* in which the word is used. For example, the word *bug* has an obvious meaning that comes to mind: a little insect. However, when presented in the following context the meaning changes: "Her little brother would *bug* her by sneaking up on her and pulling her braid." Or, " The detective placed a *bug* in the car so he could listen to the conversation while they were driving."
- We consider the meaningful word parts, or *morphemes*. For example, the meaning of the word "semicircle" can be determined when we know that semi means part or one-half.
- We combine information from our personal experience and context to interpret *figurative language*. For example, in the sentence, "Her *heart sank* when she saw that the lottery numbers did not match her selection," the person's heart does not really drop. The expression means that she was disappointed and saddened.

Context—Read the following passage. What do you think the underlined word means? What information in the context helps you figure it out?

> It was fortunate that the vendor had a box of buckshee for the children to choose from, because they did not have a single penny to spend. (Bryson, 1990, p. 237)

Buckshee is something that is free. The words that help us figure this out are "did not have a single penny to spend."

Trainer Presentation

Lesson Emphasis: We use context, morphemes, and awareness of figurative language to assist children to increase their vocabulary.

1. Read and explain each of the three bullets on this page
2. Direct participants to complete each of the brief activities for context, morphemes, and figurative language with you. Follow the directions provided in the text. (Use chart paper or transparency.)

Context: The underlined word, *buckshee*, means something that is free.

Morphemes: Write the words participants provide. List them in a column on chart paper under the morpheme *struc(t)*. Ask participants for the meaning of this morpheme; it means "build."

Figurative Language: Define figurative language using the text on this page. Explain that it is important to teach meanings of figurative language, especially to children for whom English is not their first language. Instruct participants to complete the brief exercise on the next page in small groups. Ask participants to share their responses with the whole group.

- *My stomach flipped*—"Have you ever had a scary experience? Sometimes when someone sees something kind of scary they feel a little upset stomach..."
- *...hillside sunrise*—"When the trees turn yellow, orange, and red in the fall they can sometimes look like the colors of a sunrise or sunset."

(continued)

ParaReading
A Training Guide for Tutors

Morphemes—With a partner, brainstorm as many words as you can think of that have the word part *struc(t)*. Example: instruction.

Examples may include: instruct, construct, construction, structure

Share your collection of words with your trainer.

Given the collection of words, can you guess the meaning of the morpheme *struc*? Discuss.

Figurative Language—Beautiful and interesting verbal expression is created through figurative language. It is a common tool used by authors to enrich content and individualize their writing. Adults may intuit the meaning of figurative language more easily than children. For this reason, it is important that teachers be aware of the use of figurative language in the text that children will be listening to or reading and prepare them for it. This is especially true with English-language learners.

Find the figurative language in each of the following examples. Work with your group to come up with explanations that you would provide for your students. Tip: Tie the figurative language to your own experience and help the children connect with a personal experience of their own.

My stomach flipped when I saw the cyclist approach the weakened wooden ramp at top speed.

Example: My stomach gets a tippy-turvey feeling when I sense that something unpleasant may happen.

It was a crisp autumn morning, and the sunlight transformed the reds, yellows, and oranges into a hillside sunrise.

Example: The trees' autumn colors of red, orange, and yellow made the hills look like a sunrise or sunset.

How to Teach It: Vocabulary

As a paraeducator, you can help motivate students to learn new words. The approaches described below provide simple ways to help children build interest in words and increase their understanding and use of vocabulary. Enjoy being the student as your trainer models each of the *ParaReading* vocabulary teaching components.

Choice Vocabulary—Wonder Words

Wonder Words are words or phrases (figurative language) that you anticipate may present comprehension difficulty for your students. Prepare students by *preteaching* the Wonder Words to improve the students' text comprehension.

There are two components to *ParaReading* vocabulary instruction:

- You, the tutor, choose the Wonder Words and provide definitions.
- Students use a Wonder Words journal to log the words.

Vocabulary instruction begins with finding Wonder Words in material that you will be reading to the students or that they will be reading themselves. Follow these steps:

- Preread the material that your students will be reading or that you will read to your students.
- Choose two words that meet the Wonder Words criteria: a) words or phrases that may be difficult to understand and that the students may hear or read again and therefore need to know; or b) words that may have multiple meanings.
- Provide information about the words' definitions.
- Use each word or phrase in a sentence related to the reading selection.
- Have the students tell you a sentence using each word and enter the words into their Wonder Words vocabulary journals.
- Review the Wonder Words the next time you meet with your students.

Trainer Presentation

Transparency 37a
Vocabulary Lesson: Wonder Words

Lesson Emphasis: Participants learn what Wonder Words are and learn how they can help students improve their vocabulary.

1. Tell participants that a reading tutor can help students build interest in words and increase their understanding of words and use of new vocabulary.
2. Explain to the participants: "We are using the term **Wonder Words** because there are so many words in our language that can help us 'wonder' about what we are learning. The challenge for reading tutors when teaching vocabulary is choosing the Wonder Words. You will learn to choose words to preteach prior to reading that may be difficult to understand but have high utility for children. High utility means that the child would be likely to come across the word again and would be likely to use the word in conversation."
3. Say: "Words have multiple meanings, and this poses a challenge for many of our students, especially English-language learners." The approach calls for choosing the words and preteaching them—talking about what they mean in the context of what the child reads or will have read to them.
4. Define the two components of *ParaReading* vocabulary instruction: 1) choosing Wonder Words, and 2) using a Wonder Words journal to log definitions. Present each, highlighting the information on this page that will help them understand the importance of preteaching vocabulary and how to do it.
5. Read the bulleted steps to the participants. Instruct them to follow along with you. Explain that this is a step-by-step process.

Trainer Presentation

Lesson Emphasis: Participants experience the vocabulary lesson steps.

Transparency 37b
Vocabulary Lesson: Passage

Transparency 38
Wonder Words Journal Page

1. Explain that you will follow the steps for the vocabulary lesson and instruct the participants to follow along and record the lesson content on this page.
2. Tell them that you previewed the Vocabulary Lesson: Passage (**37b**) and that you chose two Wonder Words. The first one is *latch*. Write *latch* on the first line of **Transparency 38—Wonder Words Journal Page**.
3. Provide definitions: Say, "***Latch*** is an interesting word because it can mean more than one thing. It can be a hook on a door or gate, and it can mean to remember a thought."
4. Use the word in sentences: Say, "When I want to close the gate and make sure it stays closed, I *latch* it. I *latch* it with a hook. When I want to remember something, my brain will *latch* onto the information or hook onto it so that I can keep it in my mind. I want you to *latch* onto this information about *latch* so that you can use it when we read the passage."
5. Ask participants to use latch in sentences, applying both definitions.
6. Instruct the group to write a sentence and/or draw pictures to show both meanings of *latch*. Ask individuals to share their responses.
7. **Next word**: Say, "The next Wonder Word is intrinsic. Write it on the line."
8. Provide definition: ***Intrinsic*** means something that is basic and essential to our nature.

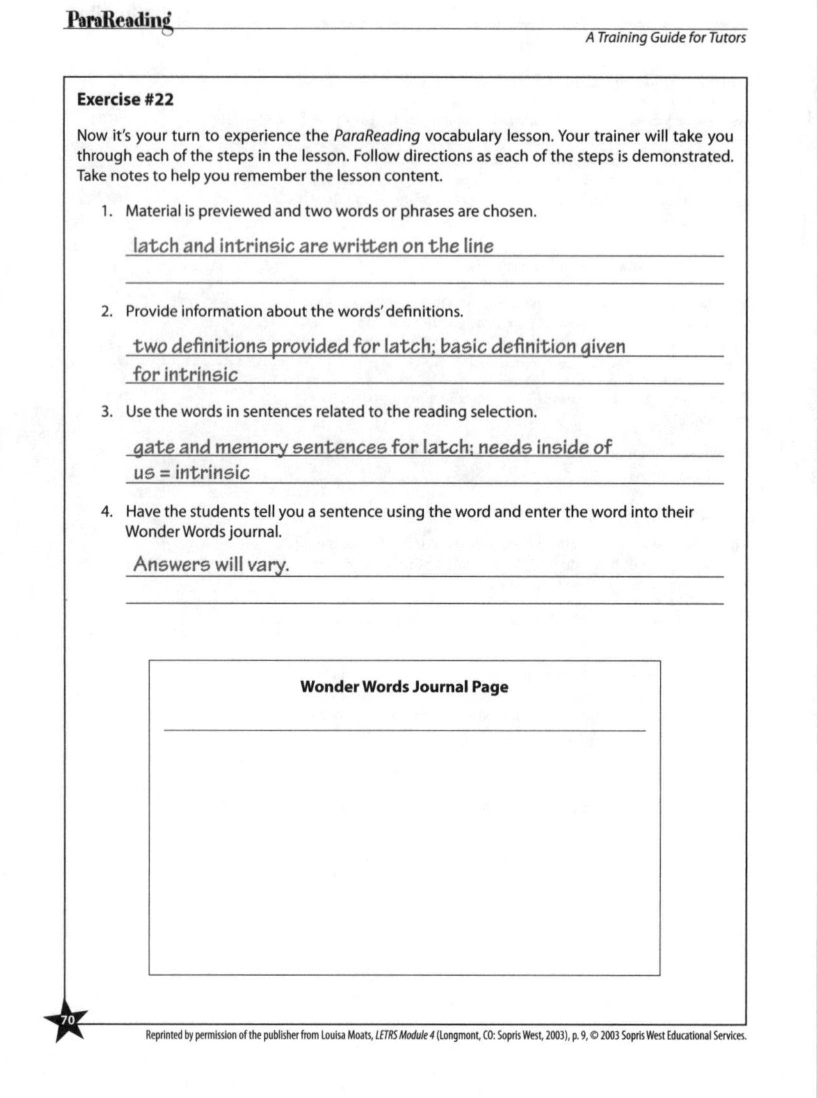
ParaReading
A Training Guide for Tutors

Exercise #22

Now it's your turn to experience the *ParaReading* vocabulary lesson. Your trainer will take you through each of the steps in the lesson. Follow directions as each of the steps is demonstrated. Take notes to help you remember the lesson content.

1. Material is previewed and two words or phrases are chosen.
   latch and intrinsic are written on the line
2. Provide information about the words' definitions.
   two definitions provided for latch; basic definition given for intrinsic
3. Use the words in sentences related to the reading selection.
   gate and memory sentences for latch; needs inside of us = intrinsic
4. Have the students tell you a sentence using the word and enter the word into their Wonder Words journal.
   Answers will vary.

Wonder Words Journal Page

70

Reprinted by permission of the publisher from Louisa Moats, *LETRS Module 4* (Longmont, CO: Sopris West, 2003), p. 9, © 2003 Sopris West Educational Services.

9. Use the word in sentences: Say, "It is *intrinsic* to want to understand what someone is saying to us. We have a need that is naturally inside of us—to communicate with others. What other needs are *intrinsic*?" Lead a brief discussion on the meaning of *intrinsic*; use the morpheme *in-*.
10. Ask participants to use *intrinsic* in sentences that show they know the meaning.
11. Instruct the group to write a sentence and/or draw pictures to show the meaning of *intrinsic*. Ask individuals to share their responses.

Read the text (from **Transparency 37b**) together, or volunteer read, choral read, or you read to them. Lead participants to reflect on how preteaching the vocabulary affected their understanding of the text.

Vocabulary expansion occurs rapidly from birth through adolescence within communicative relationships. Everyday experiences with friends, caregivers, and community members shape speech habits and knowledge of language. The human mind latches onto new words as it hears them because they are the tools of communication. Humans have an intrinsic need to understand what is said to them and to share experience through language, and the brain is biologically adapted to support language acquisition. Before school and before learning to read, children learn most of the words they know through daily oral communication with adults. Adults facilitate that process when they introduce new words in a shared experience, elaborate what a child has said, confirm and clarify the child's attempts to use new words, deliberately repeat new words in conversation, or read aloud.

Practice It: Vocabulary

Your turn to try it! Pair up with a partner; one of you will be Tutor #1, and the other will be Tutor #2. Read through your corresponding reading selection, and follow steps 1–4 to prepare for a vocabulary lesson.

Tutor #1

Beware of Bears

Bears! Many people are fascinated by them. After all, who can resist a stuffed, cuddly teddy bear? Bear enclosures at zoos are often a popular exhibit. Watching adorable bear cubs romp brings smiles and chuckles from onlookers.

1. Preread the material.
2. Choose two **Wonder Words** that may present difficulty in understanding:

   Fascinated and exhibit are two possible answers.

Trainer Presentation

Lesson Emphasis: Participants prepare and teach the *ParaReading* vocabulary process.

1. Ask participants to pair up and number as one and two.
2. Read over the directions on this page with the group. All work independently to choose their words and prepare definitions and examples from context.
3. Instruct the "ones" to get together and all "twos" to get together. Ask them to share the words they chose, to explain to each other why they chose those words and share their lesson preparation. This is outlined on the next page.

Transparency 39
Vocabulary Data Record Form

4. Show participants how to use the Vocabulary Data Recording Form. Use *latch* and *intrinsic* to show them how to record a simulated error.
5. Once they have their lessons ready and have reviewed them with their ones and twos peers, instruct the original pairs to take turns role-playing the lessons.

The lesson steps are printed on the next page. Instruct them to refer to this list and to use the Wonder Words journal page for their lesson. Each "student" should read the selection when the vocabulary instruction is completed.

(continued)

3. Provide information about the words' definitions:

   Fascinated means very interested.

   An *exhibit* is a show.

4. Provide examples of the words' usages in context:

   Possible answers: Bears fascinate me. I am very interested in the way they look. We go to the zoo to see the bear exhibit.

Data Recording—Record student performance and the Wonder Words you chose using the following form.

Vocabulary – (circle one) **Listening or Reading**
Can the student use the vocabulary words in a sentence that shows he/she knows the word? Yes No
What were the Wonder Words?

Tutor #2

> **Camels: One Hump or Two?**
> Camels are funny-looking animals with humps on their backs. Camels are large animals. They are seven or eight feet tall. They have small heads but long, curved necks. Their legs are long, but their bodies are heavy. Camels are used for riding or for carrying heavy loads.

1. Preread the material.
2. Choose two Wonder Words that may present difficulty in understanding:

   humps and *curved* are two possible answers.

ParaReading
A Training Guide for Tutors

3. Provide information about the words' definitions:

   Humps: discuss bumps, where we would see humps. Curved: Compare straight and curved.

4. Provide examples of the words' usages in context:

   Possible answers: I sat between the humps on the camel's back. The animal's neck was curved not straight.

Data Recording—Record student performance and the Wonder Words you chose using the following form.

> **Vocabulary** – (circle one) **Listening or Reading**
>
> Can the student use the vocabulary words in a sentence that shows he/she knows the word? Yes No
>
> What were the Wonder Words?

Now, #1 tutors get together, and #2 tutors get together. Compare your vocabulary choices and preparation. What are the similarities and differences? Why did you choose the words you did? Share your lesson preparations. What can we learn from each other?

OK, get back together with your partner. One of you will act as the tutor and the other as the student. Use the following guidelines to practice *ParaReading* vocabulary instruction. The tutor first writes the chosen words on the Wonder Word journal page (a reproducible version is available at the end of the workbook), and then the "student" writes sentences using the words or draws pictures of the words. Switch roles when you have successfully completed your role-play.

73

Trainer Presentation: 10 min.

Ask participants to share experiences as tutor and as student.

Discuss the differences in Wonder Word choices. Were the selected words ones that have high utility? Ones the children are apt to come across again some day? Ones they can use in their own speech?

Read aloud the ***Tip*** on this page. Tell participants to review vocabulary regularly using the Wonder Words journal.

Instruct participants to work in small groups to review this chapter for the review assessment. Tell them to review the four-part processing system; context, morphemes, and figurative language; and the Wonder Word lesson format.

Review this chapter briefly to prepare participants for the assessment.

(continued)

1. Show the written Wonder Words to the student (journal page). Read the words. "These are Wonder Words that you will be reading today."
2. Read each word and provide definitions.
3. Tell about the word using the context of the story.
4. Have the student record a picture or brief definition in the Wonder Word journal to help recall the meaning.
5. Instruct the student to read the passage.
6. Record student performance using the data form.

Tip: Revisit the Wonder Words journal and discuss the words in relation to the story. Always encourage students to use the Wonder Words in their discussion. "Tell me about it, and use the word _________." Rephrase for the students if they do not use the Wonder Words. Provide opportunities for the students to apply the vocabulary to their own experiences.

Share role-play experiences with the whole group.

ParaReading
A Training Guide for Tutors

Wonder Words

Wonder Words

75

Trainer Presentation: 20 to 30 min.

1. Direct participants to independently complete the review.
2. Gather review assessments, correct them, and record performance on the Assessment Record. Participants will want to see their assessments after you have corrected them. Make plans to return the assessments and allow for discussion.

Review: Vocabulary

1. Describe the four-part processing system. Identify the four parts and tell how they work together to help gain meaning from written text.
   The four-part processing system is made up of the Orthographic, Phonological, Meaning, and Context processors. When we read, the Orthographic processor is first to be stimulated. If we recognize the word visually (Phonological processor), we then search for the Meaning of that word and cycle it through the Context processor for full understanding.

2. Describe the process for choosing and defining the Wonder Words that you will teach your students. *Wonder Words criteria: Words or phrases that may present difficulty in understanding. Words that the child may hear or read again. Words that the child may add to their oral vocabulary. When defining Wonder Words, place them in the context of what the child will be reading and in the context of their own experience.*

3. Define *context*, and give an example of how it relates to teaching vocabulary.
   Context is the setting in which vocabulary is used. Context helps to put vocabulary and concepts that have multiple meanings into the proper perspective. Context can help us figure out the meanings of words.

ParaReading
A Training Guide for Tutors

4. Define *figurative language*, and tell how it relates to teaching vocabulary.

Figurative language is a tool used by authors to creatively describe, explain, and enrich their writing. Understanding figurative language requires the reader to think beyond the literal and interpret meaning from a basis of personal experience.

5. Define *morpheme*, and tell how morphemes relate to teaching and learning vocabulary.

A morpheme is the smallest part of a word that carries meaning. Morphemes are roots and affixes that combine to create new words. When an unfamiliar word is read, its meaning can be determined, many times, by studying its morphemes. Teaching children prefix and suffix meanings and providing examples of these morphemes in words is a good vocabulary approach because it begins an awareness of the richness of the English language.

6. What can you do to help your students remember the vocabulary you teach them?

I can revisit the words we learn often, even every week. We can review and reread them in our Wonder Word journals. I can ask the students to use the Wonder Words in sentences of their own.

Chapter 5: Comprehension

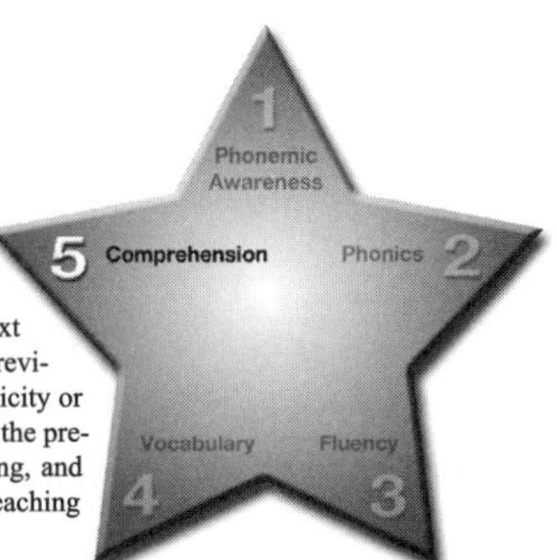

Discussion

Comprehension can be a complex process to identify and define. What does it mean to *you*? Comprehension has to do with *meaning*—deriving meaning from what we hear and what we read. Our ability to comprehend text depends on our understanding of the vocabulary, our previous experience and knowledge of the content, the simplicity or complexity of the text structure, our ability to hold onto the presented information and connect it with previous learning, and our language skills. This sounds complicated and it is! Teaching comprehension is not easy!

For many years, educators thought that comprehension happened as a natural outcome of the ability to read. We have since learned that this is not the case. Specific strategy instruction is required to teach the reader how to gain information from the text he reads, how to expand learning beyond the text, and how to combine meaning from several sources. More than likely, this intensive strategy instruction will take place within the classroom with whole-group instruction. *ParaReading* provides guidelines to help the paraeducator *support* the development of reading comprehension skills. Simple prompting or questioning before reading, during reading, and after reading can help students understand text as they read. Additionally, asking students to tell about what they have just read sends a message to students that what they are reading is important. Attending to the content and recalling the content of what they read plays an important role in comprehension.

Your Turn to Learn

You can help children improve comprehension skills when they read material or when you read to them. When children read, they exercise *reading comprehension*. When you read to children, they use *listening comprehension*. Whichever avenue a child uses to access the written material, we can use the same approach to support the development of comprehension skills. If your students have low reading skills, you may spend a portion of your time reading to them. You can use this opportunity to apply comprehension prompts. A prompt is a question or inquiry that initiates the comprehension process.

Trainer Presentation

Lesson Emphasis: Comprehension is not an easy skill to teach. We can monitor how well students comprehend by questioning them, but teaching them how to make the connections, how to understand potentially difficult language structure, is not easy. However, there are approaches that young children can use to help improve their understanding of the text they read and listen to.

Transparency 40
April Fool's Day

Complete the Exercise

Materials—Project transparency with the title covered up.

1. Ask a volunteer to read the passage aloud.
2. Ask, "What do you think this is about?" After a brief discussion, show the title. Discuss how having this information changes their understanding of the text.
3. Tell the participants that you gave them access to *background knowledge* when you showed them the title, which changed and strengthened their comprehension of the text. Ask, "How does this inform our comprehension instruction?" Explain that when we provide students with information about what they will be reading or listening to, we help them connect with previous personal experience (background knowledge) they may have with the subject matter. This strengthens comprehension.
4. Instruct them to write their answers to question 1 on the lines provided.

Transparency 41a and 41b
Airport Trauma

1. Explain that you will take the group through another reading passage, but this time you will prompt or question them to help prepare them for the passage and help them understand what they read.
2. Instruct them to listen for your prompts and record them in the blanks on this page indicating when they were used—before, during, or after reading.
3. Say, "Have you ever heard the word 'trauma'? What does it mean? Have any of you ever experienced trauma?" Show the title: Airport Trauma. "Have any of you ever been on a tight schedule with little ones in tow?" Discuss. "What do you think will happen in this story?" Discuss.
4. Instruct a volunteer to read. Stop the reader after "my heart stopped." Ask the group, "What do you think will happen next?" Discuss and ask the volunteer to read to the end.
5. Say, "Tell me about what you just read." Then, "Do you have any questions about what you just read?"
6. Instruct participants to complete questions 2–4 in their workbook. Discuss.

ParaReading
A Training Guide for Tutors

When the child reads material to you, use the same prompts to support the development of reading comprehension.

How is *your* comprehension? Let's do a little role-playing and try out a few comprehension prompts and strategies.

> **Tutors Know!** *Reading Comprehension:* understanding what we read ourselves. Listening Comprehension: understanding what someone else reads to us!

Exercise #23: Background Experience

Your trainer will show you something to read. The experience will impress you with the important role that our personal experience brings to our ability to understand what we read.

1. What happened when you first read the selection? How did that change when you saw the title of the selection? What does this mean for our students and their ability to comprehend what they read?

   Example: Participants may share that they weren't sure about what they were reading. Once they saw the title, it all made sense to them. The title gave them the information they needed to interpret the content.

2. Let's try it again with another selection. This time your trainer will prepare you for the reading, give you some background knowledge, and ask questions to help you understand the content. Record the comprehension *prompts* that are used before, during, and after the reading. A prompt is a question or inquiry that initiates the comprehension process.

   Before reading: Discussion of trauma. Asked about personal experience. Predict what will happen.

   During reading: Predict. What do you think will happen next?

   After reading: Retell. Tell me about what you just read. Do you have any questions?

ParaReading

A Training Guide for Tutors

3. Tell about your experience with comprehension *this* time. How was it different from the first reading? Which reading example were you most comfortable with as a learner?

   Answers will vary.

4. What other clues do authors provide for us that can be used to prepare young readers for what they will be reading?

   Additional clues might be pictures, subheadings, synopsis on book cover.

How to Teach It: Comprehension

Predict, Apply, Retell

You will learn how to use three strategies to help your students improve their reading comprehension:

- Predict
- Apply background knowledge (previous experience)
- Retell

These strategies are typically used before reading, during reading, and after reading. Each one has prompts or questions associated with it.

Predict:

- "Tell me what you think will happen in this story."
- "What do you think will happen next?"

Trainer Presentation

Lesson Emphasis: Introduction to the three comprehension strategies that this training prepares them to use: predict, apply background knowledge, and retell.

Trainer Presentation

Lesson Emphasis: Participants learn how to teach comprehension using the predict, background information, and retell strategies. Each strategy has its own prompt or question associated with it.

Transparency 42
Comprehension Strategies

1. Read the sample prompts for the three strategies.
2. Practice: Say the prompts randomly, and have participants give you the strategy.
3. Explain that the three strategies are typically applied before reading, while reading, and after reading.
4. Instruct participants to complete the exercise in pairs. Discuss answers as a whole group.

Read through the Error Response section. Model using a sample from the previous exercises you just completed.

Apply Background Knowledge:

- "Tell me what you know about *(fill in the blank with something from the reading selection)*."
- "Has this every happened to you?"

Retell:

- "Tell me all about what you just read."
- "Tell me two things that you learned from your reading."

Key Point: As a tutor, your role will be to hold students accountable for reading for meaning. The simple questions and prompts that you use will send the message that when we read, we read to learn something! It is important to read for meaning and to remember!

Tutors Know! Tutors ask simple questions and talk about text meaning to help children understand that we read to learn!

A Training Guide for Tutors
ParaReading

Exercise #24

Do this activity with a partner. Consider the strategies above to answer these questions.

1. Which questions or prompts could you use *before reading*?

   Tell me what you think will happen in this story. Other answers that convey prereading prompts

2. Which questions or prompts could you use *while the student is reading*?

   What do you think will happen next? Other questions reflecting appropriate during-reading dialogue.

3. Which questions or prompts could you use *when the student has finished reading*?

   Has this ever happened to you? Tell me about it. There will be other answers appropriate to post-reading comprehension checks.

Share and discuss your answers with the group.

Trainer Presentation

Prepare for the Practice Activity

Ask participants to form small groups of three or four. Direct them to work together to develop their prompts for the two stories and record the prompts in the spaces provided with each story, indicating whether the prompt will be used before, during, or after the reading. The actual role-playing practice will happen later.

Lesson Emphasis: Participants receive support while developing prompts.

1. When they are finished, direct small groups to share their prompts with the whole group (next page). Encourage participants to record additional prompts they hear.
2. Ask participants to identify generic or standard prompts that have the potential to be used again and again.

Practice It: Comprehension

You have learned three strategies that will form the basis for your focus on improving comprehension skills. Recall that comprehension is not an easy skill to teach because of the many language and processing skills that we use to gain meaning from text. The following activity will give you the opportunity to practice with your partner. You will work together to develop the prompts for each of the three strategies. Then, each of you will take a turn being the tutor or the student to try out the comprehension questions that you developed.

Read through each story together. Work together to develop your comprehension plan. Indicate whether your prompts will be used before, during, or after reading.

Story #1: Fooling Around

Rain and Wind sat resting on a mountain top. The sun was out, and there wasn't a cloud in the sky. Wind and Rain could see the people in the small town at the bottom of the mountain. Kids were playing in the park. People were sitting in the sun reading the Sunday paper. Everyone seemed happy.

Wind and Rain began to get bored because they didn't have anything to do. Wind said, "See me make the people run." Then Wind sent hats and papers flying down the street. Wind laughed, "What fun!"

Rain said, "I can make the people run too." So, Rain made black clouds. Soon big drops of water began falling. Rain laughed as the people ran for shelter.

ParaReading
A Training Guide for Tutors

(continued) **Story #1:** Fooling Around

Now develop two prompts for each strategy. For each prompt, indicate if you will use it before, during, or after reading the story.

Predict:

1. Answers will vary. Possible answers include: What do you think will happen in this story?

2. Can wind and rain talk with each other?

Apply Background Knowledge:

1. Answers will vary. Possible answers include: Have you ever been in a big wind and rain storm? Tell me about it.

2. If it is windy and rainy outside, what kinds of things do you like to do?

Retell:

1. Answers will vary. Possible answers include: Tell me all about what you just read.

2. Tell me about the wind and the rain in this story.

Trainer Presentation

Lesson Emphasis: Participants experience the process as teacher and student.

1. After participants share their prompts, instruct them to pair up and role-play the process. Tell them to use the prompts they developed.

Transparency 43
Comprehension Data Record Form

2. Demonstrate use of the Comprehension Data Record Form (next page). Talk through a possible student response and record the performance.
3. Instruct participants to use the error response strategies and data form (next page) during their lessons.

ParaReading
A Training Guide for Tutors

Story #2: A Chicken's Life

Every chicken begins life the same way—as an egg. This is what happens. A hen and rooster mate. The hen lays between seven and fifteen eggs. Then the hen sits on the eggs until they hatch.

Once the hen lays the eggs, little chicks begin to form inside each of the eggs. At the start, the chicks seem to be little red specks on the eggs. In time, the specks get bigger.

After two days, you can see the heads of the chicks forming. After seven days, you can see the beginnings of their legs and wings. The chicks keep developing. Soon you can see their beaks. All this time, the mother hen sits on her nest.

After twenty-one days in the eggs, the little chicks run out of food. They become so big that they need to get out of their shells. "Peck, peck, peck."

All chicks have a tooth, called an egg tooth. The egg tooth helps them crack their shells. When they get out, the chicks are dripping wet and not very pretty. After a short time they fluff up. Soon they can eat and get around by themselves. "Cheep, cheep, cheep." Before long, the little chicks become roosters and hens.

Tutors Know! Prompt: a prepared question or query that is used to lead discussion of a reading selection.

Now develop two prompts for each strategy. Indicate for each prompt if you will use it before, during, or after reading the story.

Predict:

1. ______________________________
____
____

2. ______________________________
____
____

ParaReading
A Training Guide for Tutors

(continued) **Story #2:** A Chicken's Life

Apply Background Knowledge:

1. Before—Have you ever hatched eggs in your classroom?
2. During—What do you know about baby chicks hatching from their eggs?

Retell:

1. After—Tell me something you remember about the story.
2. After—Tell me what it is like for the baby chick when it hatches out of its egg.

Share your prompts with the group. How do they compare? Do you hear other prompts that you would like to use? Write them here:

Use your prepared prompts to role-play student and tutor. When you are the tutor, record student successes and/or any concerns you may have with your student's responses.

Trainer Presentation

Lesson Emphasis: Review the three strategies and the development of prompts. Distinguish between listening and reading comprehension. Prepare for assessment.

1. Ask participants to share their experiences using the prompts they prepared.
2. Review Error Response section.
3. Explain that the *ParaReading* training is now complete. Tell them that the remainder of their manual covers additional instructional tips and information that is important to their work. Tutor's Tips provides a wealth of information to help reading tutors with organizing, communicating, and building positive relationships with students.
4. Ask participants to form small groups and review the material in this comprehension chapter. Tell them to be ready to write about the strategies, know how to respond to errors, and provide prompts.

The information in Tutor's Tips can be presented in a separate follow-up training, or at the close of the comprehension chapter.

Direct them to Tutor's Tips for Strategy Reference Cards that will serve as reminders and supports as they teach the five components of effective reading!

Error Response

If your student is having difficulty with comprehension try the following:

- Model or show the student your thinking out loud as you answer the question or prompt. Then, ask the student to respond again: "Now you try." Ask the question again.
- On your data sheet, note the difficulty your student is having and share this information with your supervising teacher. Ask if there is anything else the teacher would like you to do during your tutor sessions to help improve comprehension.

Data Recording

Comprehension—*(circle one)* **Listening or Reading**

Student does this well: *(circle)*

predicts, applies background knowledge, retells

Student has difficulty with / I had to help the student with:

Discuss your teaching comprehension experiences with your group and trainer. Your trainer will help you prepare for the chapter assessment.

ParaReading
A Training Guide for Tutors

Review: Comprehension

1. What are three comprehension strategies that you can use to increase reading comprehension?
   Predict
   Apply background knowledge
   Retell

2. At what times during a student's reading will you apply your comprehension instruction?
   Before reading
   During reading
   After reading

3. What is the difference between listening comprehension and reading comprehension?
   Listening comprehension is the meaning that children attend to when the information is read to them.
   Reading comprehension is the meaning that children attend to when they read the information themselves.

4. What is a prompt? Give three examples of prompts, one for each strategy covered in the lesson.
   A prompt is a carefully developed question or statement that initiates a discussion about text. It can prepare students for reading material by helping them access background knowledge or by creating new background knowledge.
   Examples will vary but should reflect the questions that were used in the activities and text examples.
   PREDICT: Tell me what you think will happen in this story.
   What do you think will happen next?
   BACKGROUND KNOWLEDGE: Tell me what you know about (fill in the blank with something from the reading selection.)
   Has this every happened to you?
   What do you already know about (fill in the blank with something from the reading selection)?
   RETELL: Tell me all about what you just read.
   Tell me two things that you learned from your reading.

89

Trainer Presentation: 20 to 30 min.

1. Direct participants to independently complete the review.
2. Gather review assessments, correct them, and record performance on the Assessment Record. Participants will want to see their assessments after you have corrected them. Make plans to return the assessments and allow for discussion.

ParaReading
A Training Guide for Tutors

(continued) **Review:** Comprehension

5. How will you respond if your student has difficulty or makes an error?

Model or show the student your thinking out loud as you answer the question or prompt. Then ask the student to respond again: "Now you try." Then ask the question again.

On your data sheet, note the difficulty your student is having and share this information with your supervising teacher. Ask if there is anything else the teacher would like you to do during your tutoring sessions to help improve comprehension.

Four-Part Processing System–An Overview

Trainers: It is critical that you have an understanding of the four-part processing system prior to teaching the vocabulary chapter. Please read through this section several times before you teach it.

That reading depends on the coordinated use of multiple brain systems suggests a well-documented inference: Reading problems may originate in any or all of the processing systems. Subtypes of poor readers may have specific problems in one of these processing systems. If reading instruction is well designed it will educate all of the functions: recognition and fast processing of sounds, letters patterns, morphemes, word meanings, phrases, sentences, and longer passages.

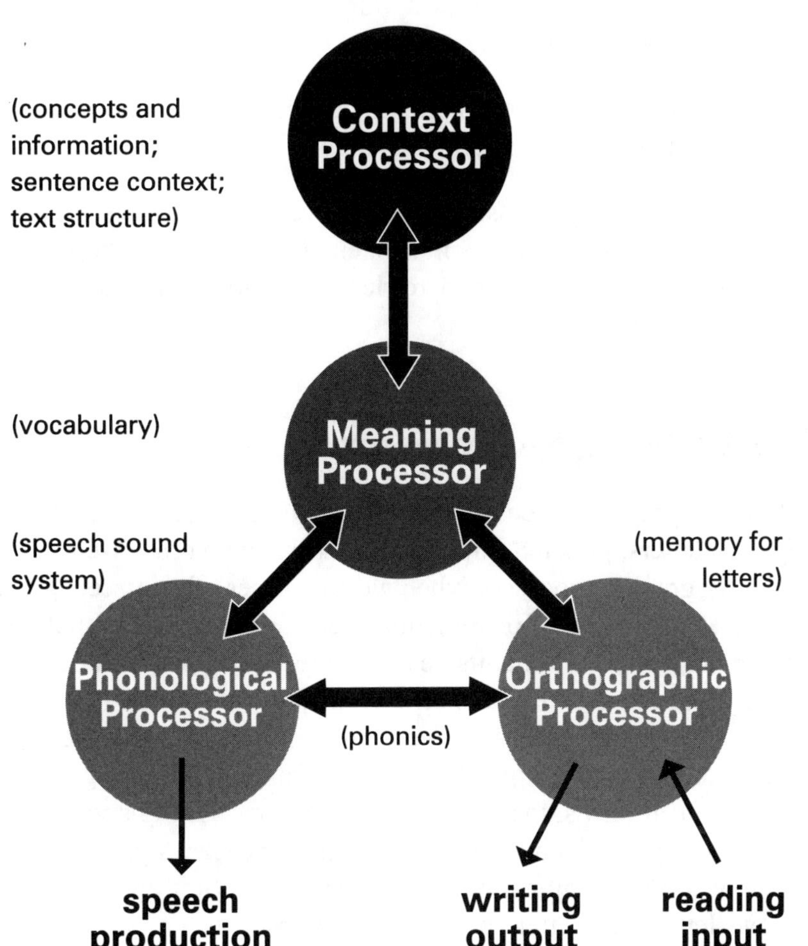

Reprinted by permission of the publisher from Louisa Moats, *LETRS: Module 1* (Longmont, CO: Sopris West, 2005), p. 24, © 2005 by Sopris West.

The Phonological Processor

This network enables us to perceive, remember, interpret, and produce the speech sound system of our own language and learn the sounds of other languages. The phonological processor allows us to imitate and produce stress patterns, including the rise and fall of the voice during phrasing. It is responsible for such functions as:

- Establishing identities for the phoneme or distinguishing speech sounds in a language.
- Remembering the words in a phrase or the sounds in a word.
- Comparing words that sound similar, such as *reintegrate* and *reiterate*.
- Retrieving specific words from the mental dictionary (lexicon) and producing the speech sounds.
- Holding the sounds of a word in memory so that a word can be written down.
- Taking apart the sounds in a word so that they can be matched with alphabetic symbols.

The phonological processor detects, stores, and retrieves the phonemes and sound sequences in spoken language; the orthographic processor detects, stores and retrieves the graphemes and letter sequences in print.

The Orthographic Processor

The orthographic processing system visually perceives and recognizes letters, punctuation marks, spaces, and words. We rely on the orthographic processor when we copy lines of print, recognize words as whole units, or remember letter sequences for spelling. When we look at print, its features are filtered, identified, and matched to images of letters or letter sequences already in memory. If the letters or letter sequences are familiar, we associate them with sounds and meanings. We have no trouble interpreting widely varying print forms, including individual handwriting styles, type fonts, or uppercase and lowercase letters. The size, style, and case of print are not major factors in word recognition once a reader knows letters and letter-sound relationships.

The orthographic processing system stores information about print necessary for word recognition and for spelling. The speed with which letters are recognized and recalled is very important for proficient reading. Obviously, print images must be associated with meaning for reading comprehension to occur.

The Meaning Processor

According to the four-part processing model, recognizing words as meaningful entities requires communication between the phonological processor, orthographic processor, and meaning processor. The meaningless association of speech sounds with print may allow us to "read" a foreign language without knowing what it means, to read nonsense words, or to read a new name by sounding it out, but unless the meaning processor is accessed, no comprehension is possible. The meaning processor stores the inventory of known words and also constructs the meanings of any new words that are named during reading. The context of the passage supports the construction of those meanings.

A word filed in the mental dictionary is multidimensional; its image has sound, spelling, morphological structure, and a syntactic role. The meaning processor is structured according to a number of semantic organization features, such as synonym relationships, roots and other morphemes, spelling patterns, common meaning associations, and connotations. It expands and reorganizes itself as new vocabulary is learned.

The Context Processor

The context processor influences the meaning processor in many ways. The context in which a word occurs is the sentence and sentence sequence in which it is embedded. The context provides the referent for a word's meaning. For example, many words have multiple meanings but only one is used within a specific sentence. The spelling of a word such as *passed* or *past* is determined by its meaning in the context of a sentence:

- Fielder *passed* the ball to the wide receiver for the touchdown.

Context helps us rapidly find a meaning in our mental dictionary once a word has been named:

- The idea provided a *segue* between the introduction and the body of the speech.

Context has only a very limited role in facilitating word naming itself. Word recognition and pronunciation are primarily the job of the phonological and orthographic processors.

References

Adams, G., & Brown, S. (2004). *Six-minute solution: A reading fluency program*. Longmont, CO: Sopris West Educational Services.

Adams, M. J. (1990). *Beginning to read: Thinking and learning about print*. Cambridge, MA: MIT Press.

Biemiller, A. (1999). Language and reading success. In J. Chall (Ed.), *From Reading Research to Practice: A Series for Teachers*. Cambridge, MA: Brookline Books.

Bryson, B. (1990). *The mother tongue: English and how it got that way*. New York: Harper Collins.

Cohen, P. A., Kulik, J. A., & Kulik, C. C. (1982). Educational outcomes of tutoring: A meta-analysis of findings. *American Educational Research Journal, 19*, 237–248.

Edformation (2002). *AIMSWeb Benchmark Assessments*. Available at: www.edformation.com.

Elbaum, B., Vaughn, S., Hughes, M. T., & Moody, S. W. (2000). How effective are one-on-one tutoring programs in reading for elementary students at risk for reading failure? A meta-analysis of the intervention research. *Journal of Educational Psychology*, *92*(4), 605–619.

Fitzgerald, J. (2001). Can minimally trained college student volunteers help young at-risk children read better? *Reading Research Quarterly*, *36*(1), 28–47.

Foorman, B. R., Francis, D. J., Fletcher, J. M., Schatschneider, C., & Mehta, P. (1998). The role of instruction in learning to read: Preventing reading failure in at-risk children. *Journal of Educational Psychology*, *90*(1), 37–55.

Glaser, D. R. (2002). *High school tutors: Their impact on elementary students' reading fluency through implementing a research-based instruction model*. Doctoral Dissertation: Boise State University.

Hasbrouk, J. E., Ihnot, C., & Rogers, G. (1999). Read naturally: A strategy to increase oral reading fluency. *Reading Research Instruction*, *39*(1), 27–37.

Moats, L. C. (2003). *The speech sounds of English: A video tutorial with Louisa Moats*. Longmont, CO: Sopris West Educational Services.

Moats, L. C. (1999). *Teaching reading is rocket science: What expert teachers of reading should know and be able to do.* Washington, DC: American Federation of Teachers.

Moats, L. C. (1999–2004). *Language essentials for teachers of reading and spelling* (LETRS). Longmont, CO: Sopris West Educational Services.

Moats, L. C. (2005). *Language essentials for teachers of reading and spelling* (LETRS) *Module one.* Presenter's CD-ROM by Carol Tolman. Longmont, CO: Sopris West Educational Services.

Mueser, K. T., Yarnold, P. R., & Foy, D. W. (1991). Statistical analysis for single-case designs: Evaluating outcome of imaginal exposure treatment of chronic PTSD. *Behavior Modification*, *15*(2), 134–155.

Nagy, W. E., & Anderson, R. C. (1984). How many words are there in printed school English? *Reading Research Quarterly*, *19*(3), 304-330.

No child left behind act of 2001: Executive summary. Washington, DC: U.S. Department of Education

Report of the National Reading Panel: Teaching children to read. (2000). Washington, DC: National Institutes of Health.

Shaywitz, S. (2003). *Overcoming dyslexia: A new and complete science-based program for reading problems at any level.* New York: Alfred A. Knopf.

Shinn, M. R., Deno, S. L., & Fuchs, L. S. (2002). *Using curriculum-based measurements in a problem-solving model.* New York: Guilford.

Sprick, M., Howard, L. M., & Fidanque, A. (1999). *Read Well.* Longmont, CO: Sopris West Educational Services.

U.S. Department of Education, (1999). Unpublished tabulations from the follow-up survey of state implementation of federal elementary and secondary education programs. In *The Jossey-Bass Reader on School Reform*. San Francisco; Jossey-Bass.

Vadasy, P. F., Jenkins, J. R., & Pool, K. (2000). Effects of tutoring in phonological and early reading skills on students at risk for reading disabilities. *Journal of Learning Disabilities*, *33*(4), 579–590.

Vellutino, F. R., & Scanlon, D. M. (1987). Phonological coding, phonological awareness, and reading ability: Evidence from a longitudinal and experimental study. *Merrill-Palmer Quarterly*; *33*(3), 321–63.

Wasik, B. A. (1998). Volunteer tutoring programs in reading; A review. *Reading Research Quarterly*, *33*(3), 266–292.

Blackline Masters

for Transparencies

Blackline Masters for Transparencies Contents

Paraeducators will:

- Understand the important roles that phonemic awareness, phonics, fluency, vocabulary, and comprehension have in reading instruction.
- Understand how to apply systematic and direct practices to teach students the five basic components of reading.
- Acquire specific instructional, record-keeping, and tutorial management skills.

Paraeducators will:

- Observe modeling of instructional techniques and instructional content and participate in role-playing during the training.
- Demonstrate mastery of the explicit systematic learning that strengthens effective reading instruction.
- Deliver praise, encouragement, positive feedback, and reinforcement as part of their successful instruction.

- Recognize areas in which students need extra help, and understand the importance of communicating observations to supervisors when there are questions or concerns.
- Utilize error-correction procedures that are quick, simple, and consistently applied.
- Keep accurate records as an assessment of a student's progress, of their work, and for program evaluation.

Integrated, Comprehensive Reading Instruction

1 Phonemic Awareness

2 Phonics

3 Fluency

4 Vocabulary

5 Comprehension

- **Discussion**—Each chapter begins with a discussion of the focus component. Your trainer will present background information and research, so that you will understand the importance of the skill being taught.
- **Your Turn to Learn**—Your Turn to Learn provides opportunities for you to practice and perfect your own reading skills in the area of focus. Paraeducators may have their skills assessed during this section.

- **How to Teach It**—Procedures for teaching the focus skill are presented in this section. Necessary instructional materials are listed, and a data collection process is described.

- **Practice It**—Before you teach any reading skill, you should have lots of practice! The training allows time to observe, practice in pairs, and role-play with other tutors and the trainer.

- **Review**—A brief review assessment completes each chapter. These reviews are meant to provide helpful feedback to you and your trainer as you progress through the training.

Consonant Sounds			Vowel Sounds		
1.	/b/	butter	26.	/e/	see
2.	/p/	pet	27.	/ĭ/	sit
3.	/m/	mouse	28.	/a/	make
4.	/f/	fuzz	29.	/ĕ/	bed
5.	/v/	vest	30.	/ă/	cat
6.	/th/	think	31.	/i/	time
7.	/<u>th</u>/	them	32.	/ŏ/	fox
8.	/t/	tiger	33.	/ŭ/	cup
9.	/d/	desk	34.	/aw/	saw, call, water, bought
10.	/n/	nose	35.	/o/	vote
11.	/s/	smile	36.	/oo/	book
12.	/z/	zipper	37.	/u/	tube, moo
13.	/sh/	ship	38.	/ə/ (schwa)	about, lesson
14.	/zh/	measure	39.	/oi/	oil, boy
15.	/ch/	chair	40.	/ou/	out, cow
16.	/j/	judge	41.	/er/	her, fur, sir
17.	/k/	kite	42.	/ar/	car
18.	/g/	goat	43.	/or/	corn
19.	/ng/	sang			
20.	/y/	yellow			
21.	/wh/	whistle			
22.	/w/	wagon			
23.	/h/	hand			
24.	/l/	lion			
25.	/r/	rose			

Consonant Phonemes by Place and Manner of Articulation

	Lips	Teeth/ Lips	Tongue/ Teeth	Ridge/ Teeth	Roof Mouth	Back of Throat	Glottis
Stops (Unvoiced / Voiced)	/p/ /b/			/t/ /d/		/k/ /g/	
Nasals	/m/			/n/		/ng/	
Fricatives (Unvoiced / Voiced)		/f/ /v/	/th/ /th/	/s/ /z/	/sh/ /zh/		
Affricates (Unvoiced / Voiced)					/ch/ /j/		
Glides (Unvoiced / Voiced)					/y/	/wh/ /w/	/h/
Liquids				/l/ /r/			

8 LETRS Vowel Chart

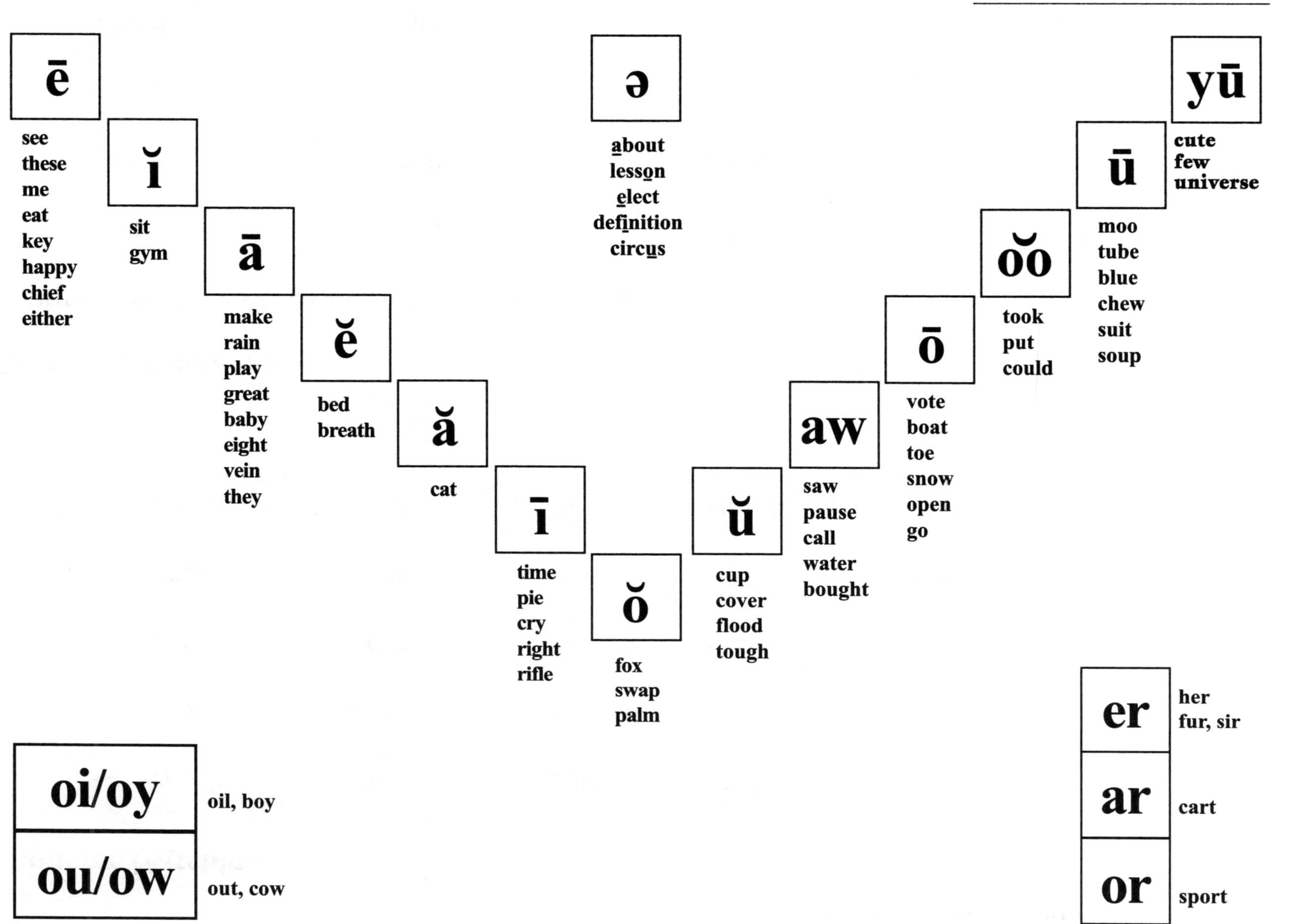

Phoneme Matching

1.	**hook**	food	cloud	foot	sugar
2.	**laugh**	faun	train	sauce	grand
3.	**miss**	does	nose	box	close
4.	**cage**	gym	game	gnat	hang
5.	**think**	blunt	sling	drink	hang

Count the Phonemes

Count the number of phonemes in the following words:

through ________	loose ________	fox ________	knight ________
high ________	pitcher ________	judge ________	fir ________
pay ________	torch ________	strong ________	oil ________
wheat ________	quiet ________	vision ________	cream ________

Identification of Phonemes

Identify the third phoneme in the following words:

shoes ________	square ________	notched ________
night ________	vision ________	square ________
sing ________	odor ________	walk ________

Segmenting Phonemes

11 *Choose Your Words*

waist flap at graft chief shift

fact night moist pup broil froze swift

2 or 3 Sounds	Initial Blends	Ending Blends	Initial and Ending Blends	Vowel Teams

1. Point out one thing that was done correctly.

2. Demonstrate the correct way.

3. Point out the place where a correction was made. Explain.

4. Student does it again with you.

Phonemic Awareness

Provide words when discussing errors

1. Student does this well: (circle)

   initial   ending   middle   segmentation   blending

2. Student errors: (circle)

   initial   ending   middle   segmentation   blending

3. Sound confusion?

Word-Play Exercises

- *Isolate First Sounds*: Say the word and ask student to say the word and the first sound in that word. Repeat the word and sound with the student.
- *Isolate Last Sounds*: Say the word and ask the student to say the word and the last sound in that word. Repeat the word and the sound with the student.
- *Isolate Middle Sounds*: Say the word and ask the student to say the word and the middle sound in that word. Repeat the word and the sound with the student. Make sure that the words you choose for this have a distinguishable middle sound. Three-sound words work best.
- *Segment All Sounds in a Word*: Say a word and ask student to tell you all of the little sounds in that word.
- *"Secret" Language (Auditory Blending)*: Say a word segmented into its isolated sounds, and have the student say the "secret word" back to ou.

Multisensory Cues

- *Tap the Sounds*: Beginning with your index finger, tap with your thumb and move through each finger, tapping once for each sound.
- *Tap Head, Waist, Ankles*: To help students isolate middle sounds, use three-sound words and tap your head for the first sound, your waist for the middle sound, and then reach down to your feet for the last sound.
- *Finger Count*: Count and say the sounds one at a time, raising a finger for each one.
- *Pull the Sounds Out of Your Mouth*: Starting at your lips, pretend to grasp each isolated sound as you move your thumb and forefinger in a pulling movement away from your mouth.
- *Use Manipulatives*: Little crackers, paper squares, or game pieces make good visuals that can help young children see the segmentation as they separate the sounds in words.

With phonics, we teach children to match letters to sounds:

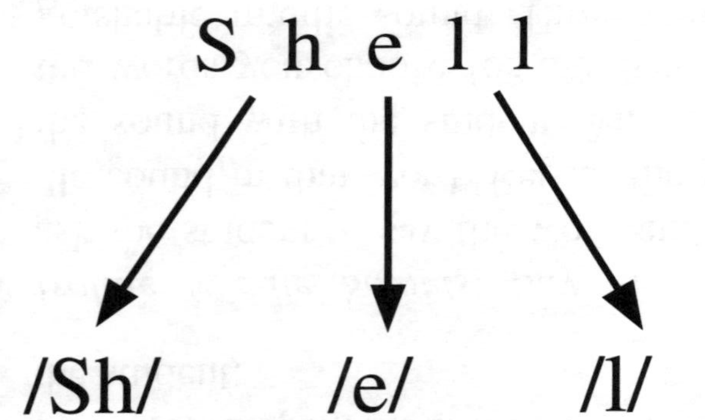

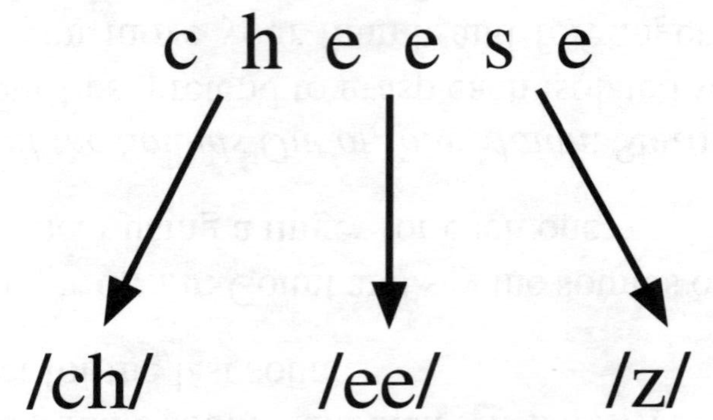

16 Grid One Empty

a apple	e echo	i itch	o octopus	u up		
a-e babe	i-e hive	o-e rose	u-e tube	u-e mule	e-e theme	
m man	p pump	s sun	b boy	t tame	d dog	f fun
l lap	r rabbit	n nose	w wish	h hair	c cat	k kite
j jam	g goat	g gym	c city	y yummy	v valentine	z zipper
qu quilt	x box					
ir shirt	er sister	ur burp	ar arm	or corn		
au autumn	aw awesome	ai sail	ay day	ee bee	oa boat	oi oil
oy joy	ea See LETRS Vowel Chart	ou See LETRS Vowel Chart	ow See LETRS Vowel Chart	oo See LETRS Vowel Chart	ew chew	
th thin	th them	sh shoe	ch chin	ng ring		

o	u	g	m	s	l	b		
oo	i	ur	aw	l	s	n	p	
o	i	ee	ng	th	s	l	n	sh

Single vowel spellings: **o, u, i**

Consonants: **n, b, g, l, s, m, p**

Digraphs: **th, ng, sh**

Vowel spellings: **aw, oo, ur, ee**

Set One: o, u, g, m, s, l, b

Set Two: oo, i, ur, aw, l, s, n, p

Set Three: o, i, ee, ng, th, s, l, n, sh

20 Nonsense Words

vog	tel	ut
zek	zub	pef
trum	blesh	splin
gake	pune	lete
tark	yort	mir
soik	zail	shay
quawp	woam	prew

Example	Level
The dish was full of shiny shells. The shrimp did not shed their shells, so there were no shrimp shells to show them.	paragraph
The ship went to find big shells under the water.	sentence
ship, dish	words
sh written	grapheme
/sh/	sound

Another name for this procedure is *touch and say*. Children touch each letter (or grapheme), say the sounds, and then blend the sounds to read the word.

Step-by-step procedure for decoding *shack*:

1. Point to the digraph *sh* at the beginning of *shack*. Say "Sound"; students say "/sh/."

2. Touch each successive grapheme, saying "Sound" for each one, /sh/ /a/ /k/, as the children make the sound that each grapheme stands for. Then, go back and blend the whole word smoothly, running your finger under the word left to right, at the rate of about one phoneme each half second.

   Continuous sounds are easier to begin with. For example, *bat* /b/ /a/ /t/ and *check* /ch/ /e/ /ck/ are a little harder than *shell*, *thin*, or *moss*.

3. Slowly compress the extended word. Go from *shshshaaack* to *shshaack* to *shack*.

4. Point to the word and say, "The word is shack."

5. Check for understanding and the ability to use the word in a phrase.

23 *Stretch-and-Say Blending*

Phonemes are segmented and counted, and then the whole word is blended with an accompanying gesture to pull the sounds together into the word.

Step-by-step procedure for decoding *sun*:

1. Say the whole word, "Sun."
2. Ask students to hold up one finger for each sound they hear as the word is segmented and the phonemes counted.
3. Say the whole word while pulling your arm down or sweeping it across your body from left to right.

Step-by-step procedure for decoding *stick*:

In unison, the tutor and student tap index finger and thumb together as they say each sound in the word and blend the sounds together. If needed, the tutor can touch each grapheme as the student taps the sounds.

1. Tap and say "/s/."
2. Tap and say "/t/."
3. Tap and say "/ĭ/."
4. Tap and say "/k/."
5. Run finger under whole word, and say, "Stick."

Decoding *book*:

1. Tutor says, “Book.”
2. Student repeats the word and moves markers into boxes for each separate sound, saying the sounds as the markers are touched and moved—“/b/ /ŏŏ/ /k/.”
3. The tutor asks two types of questions about the sounds: “Show me the /k/”, and then, pointing to the second sound marker, “What is this sound?” Student says, “/ŏŏ/.” These two questions can be repeated for different sounds in the word so that the student is responding to questions about all of the represented sounds.
4. Once the questions have been asked, the student is instructed to push up the markers one at a time and write the graphemes for each sound in the spaces, saying the sounds as the letters are written.
5. The student then writes the entire word on the line.

26 Sounds to Spelling Form

Student: ______________________

____

____

____

Decoding

Provide words when discussing errors

1. *Student does this well:*

2. *Student errors:*

3. *Sound confusion?*

28 *Eye-Voice Span Passage for Fluency Exercise*

Effective reading instruction enables students to read with comfort, concentration, and comprehension. A productive, satisfying reading experience, in turn, is associated with reading fluency. If students are taught the component skills of reading, including phonics, phonological processing, vocabulary meanings, and comprehension strategies, they will be successful readers only when their text reading is proficient enough to support comprehension. Reading fluency depends on the development of many underlying processes that must be so well learned that they can be carried out effortlessly while the mind devotes itself to making meaning.

Automaticity refers to the learned capacity to use a skill on demand without having to think it through or use up valuable attention resources. The brain has only a limited amount of "desk space" or attention capacity at any one time. Almost all complex behaviors that humans master include a set of underlying subskills that have been learned to an automatic level so that attention is devoted to higher goals. Great basketball coaches ask their players to practice and master ball handling, footwork, court coverage, and other skills until they can use them instantly in the service of complex plays. Pianists learn finger positions, keys, scales, chords and other aspects of musicianship before and during their mastery of challenging compositions. Readers must learn to recognize words accurately and quickly, so that attention can be allocated to comprehension and strategic reading for varied purposes.

30 *Fluency Training: Repeated Readings Chart*

Student Name: ______________________________

	Date: ____________ Reading Selection: ____________ ____________			Date: ____________ Reading Selection: ____________ ____________			Date: ____________ Reading Selection: ____________ ____________			
Words Read Correctly Per Minute										
120										120
100										100
90										90
80										80
70										70
60										60
50										50
40										40
30										30
20										20
10										10
0										0
	1	2	3	1	2	3	1	2	3	

Instruct the student: "Please read this passage for your fluency training today. Begin reading here (point) and read until I tell you to stop. If you come to a word you don't know, I will tell you the word." Time him for one minute, and note the number of words he reads. Subtract the errors for a total of words read correct per minute (WCPM).

1. Chart the WCPM on the Fluency Training: Repeated Readings Chart. Show the student how to graph his own performance.
2. Review the errors with the student. Show and tell him the words you helped him with, words he omitted or substituted, and words he hesitated with.
3. Instruct the student to read the passage again and follow the same procedure.
4. Do this for a total of three times, marking the errors with a different color each time. Have the student graph his performance after each reading. Work with the student to set goals between readings—"How many words can you read next time? Can you beat your time?"

There are many plants on our earth. Plants can be big. Plants can be small. We can't even see some plants. They are too small. Plants need many things to grow. They need sunlight. Some plants need a lot of sunlight. Others need very little sunlight. Some plants need a lot of water. Other plants need very little water. A cactus can live without a lot of water.

Plants also need food from the soil to grow. Plants use their roots to get food and water from the soil. The roots also hold up the plant. The leaves make food for the plant. They use the sun to make food. Stems are different on plants. The stems hold up the leaves and flowers on the plant. It also carries water and food to the plant. The stem of a tree is hard and strong. The stem of a flower can bend easily. Plants have seeds to grow new plants. Some seeds are very small. Other seeds are in fruit that grows on the plants. Some plants have flowers. Other plants do not have flowers. Plants give us many things. They are good to us.

All About Plants

There are many plants on our earth. Plants can be big. Plants can be 14
small. We can't even see some plants. They are too small. Plants need many 28
things to grow. They need sunlight. Some plants need a lot of sunlight. 41
Others need very little sunlight. Plants need water to grow. Just like 54
sunlight, some plants need a lot of water. Other plants need very little 67
water. A cactus can live without a lot of water. 77

Plants also need food from the soil to grow. Plants use their roots to 91
get food and water from the soil. The roots also hold up the plant. The 106
leaves make food for the plant. They use the sun to make food. Stems are 121
different on plants. The stems hold up the leaves and flowers on the plant. It 136
also carries water and food to the plant. The stem of a tree is hard and 152
strong. The stem of a flower can bend easily. Plants have seeds to grow new 167
plants. Some seeds are very small. Other seeds are in fruit that grows on the 182
plants. Some plants have flowers. Other plants do not have flowers. Plants 194
give us many things. They are good to us. 203

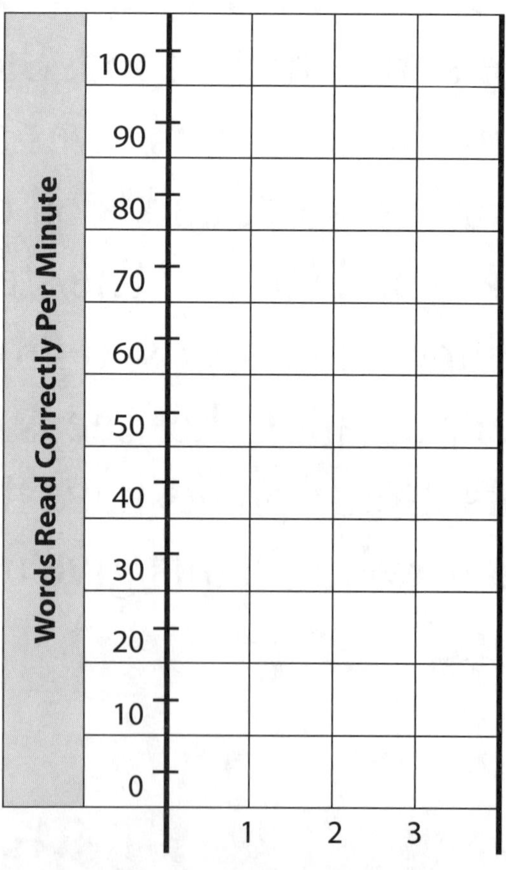

32b Repeated Readings Chart, Single

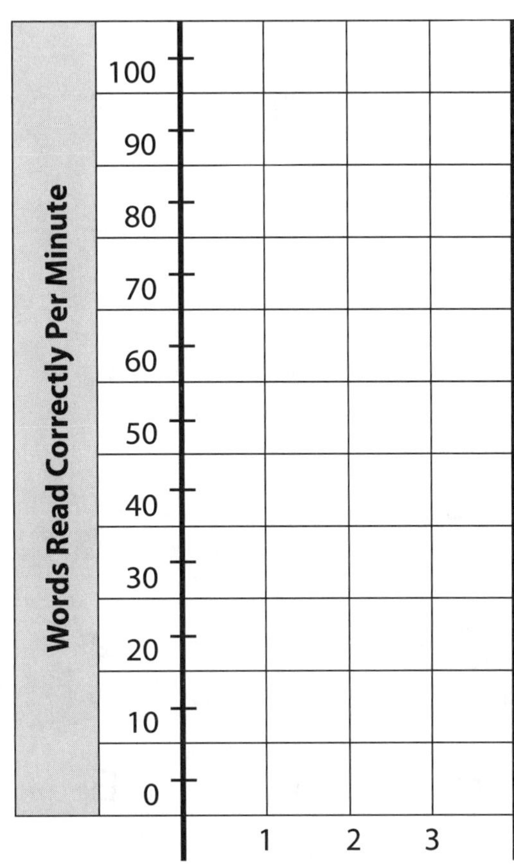

33 Grapheme Sounds

i	th	g	l	s	b	h	g	w	sh	a	u	12
H	f	x	e	a	ch	p	n	t	o	v	m	24
p	qu	s	y	n	c	d	j	r	sh	d	y	36
b	e	th	z	m	k	l	x	a	n	i	p	48
r	ch	s	y	t	th	qu	f	v	g	d	e	60

34 *Isolated Words*

fed	cut	fed	kid	then	pan	6
net	path	wet	fad	rut	lop	12
then	wet	kip	dub	that	fat	18
rug	that	bag	peg	rug	let	24
pen	bath	than	fed	did	log	30
thin	dad	fad	thin	bath	fell	36
bib	this	peg	path	pen	that	42
rut	kid	keg	net	get	pill	48
did	that	jam	bib	dad	dug	54
get	gum	kit	wet	cut	lid	60

A History of Flight: Hot Air Balloons

For thousands of years, people dreamed of traveling in the air like birds. The only 15
problem was, people had no way to fly. Then, about two hundred years ago, two French 31
brothers made a big balloon. They lit a small fire under the balloon and watched as the 49
balloon rose in the air. Their balloon was flying! 57

Would you like to understand how the hot air balloon could fly? Hot air is lighter 73
than cold air. When the brothers lit the fire, as the air got hotter, it got lighter, and the 92
balloon began to fly. What do you think happened when the air in the balloon got cold? 109

The brothers put a rooster, a sheep, and a duck on the first flight of their balloon. 126
Before long, many people rode in hot air balloons. 135

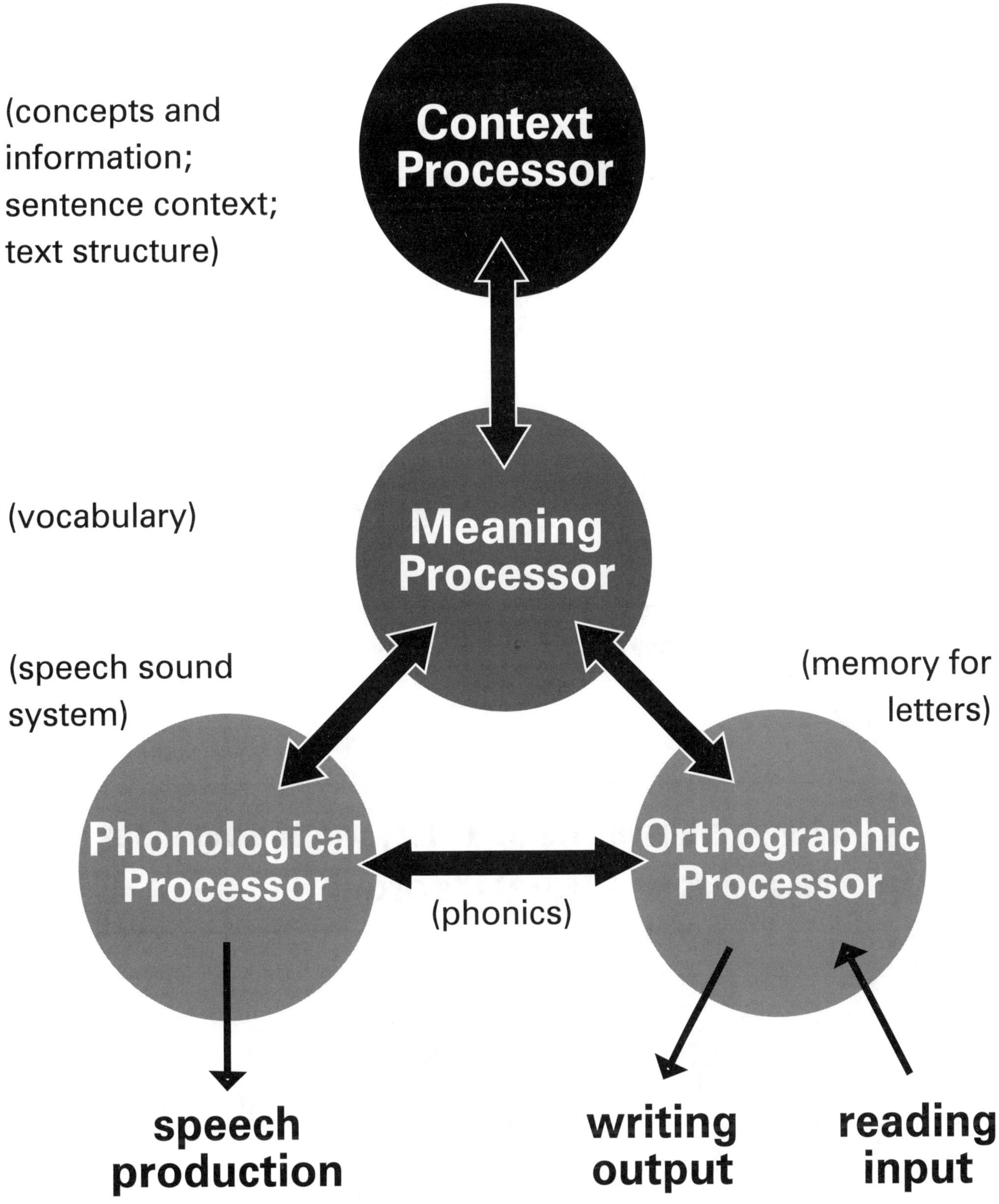

36a Four-Part Processing System

(concepts and information; sentence context; text structure)

Context Processor

(vocabulary)

Meaning Processor

(speech sound system)

(memory for letters)

Phonological Processor

Orthographic Processor

(phonics)

speech production

writing output

reading input

Letters and shapes of letters used to spell these words:

Cut separately

c	l	ow	n	clown

cloud	c	l	ou	d

Sounds for the two words:

/c/	/l/	/ow/	/n/	/d/	/s/	/z/

Cut separately

Text strip:	**A funny man who wears a fuzzy wig and big shoes who makes me laugh at the circus."**

Text strip:	**Fluffy white shapes in the sky.**

Vocabulary instruction begins with finding **Wonder Words** in reading material that you will be reading to the students or material that they will be reading. Follow these steps:

- Preread the material that your student will be reading or that you will read to your student.
- Choose two words that meet the Wonder Words criteria: a) words or phrases that may present difficulty in understanding and that the child may hear or read again and therefore need to know; or b) words that may have multiple meanings.
- Provide information about the words' definitions.
- Use each word or phrase in a sentence related to the reading selection.
- Have the student tell you a sentence using each word and enter the words into their Wonder Words vocabulary journals.
- Review the Wonder Words the next time you meet with your students.

Vocabulary expansion occurs rapidly from birth through adolescence within communicative relationships. Everyday experiences with friends, caregivers, and community members shape speech habits and knowledge of language. The human mind latches onto new words as it hears them because they are the tools of communication. Humans have an intrinsic need to understand what is said to them and to share experience through language, and the brain is biologically adapted to support language acquisition. Before school and before learning to read, children learn most of the words they know through daily oral communication with adults. Adults facilitate that process when they introduce new words in a shared experience, elaborate what a child has said, confirm and clarify the child's attempts to use new words, deliberately repeat new words in conversation, or read aloud.

Wonder Words

Vocabulary – (circle one) **Listening or Reading**

Can the student use the vocabulary words in a sentence that shows he/she knows the word?

Yes No

What were the Wonder Words?

April Fool's Day

The first step was to replace the salt in the salt shaker with sugar. Next, she loosened the light bulbs from their sockets. Following this action, she emptied the milk carton and filled it with water. As if this wasn't enough, she released the spiders that her friends had captured into the drawer.

Airport Trauma

The day had progressed well. One down and one to go. Handling this potentially challenging task by myself had not been my first choice, but it was one that could not be avoided. Another mission for Wonder Woman! We stopped and got a few snacks, some yogurt and cookies, to eat while we were waiting. I pushed the stroller, and my toddler walked along holding his yogurt. The pace was relaxing; this was not as bad as I thought it would be, and I was actually humming. Stopping to make a final check on the plan, I set down my heavy bag, rounded up the toddler, and began the search through layer after layer of necessary kid-articles for the critical piece of paper. Finding it and searching for the pertinent line of information seemed to take forever as I scattered items all around me, kept an eye on a wandering toddler, and began soothing the start of a whiny crescendo coming from the stroller. My eyes scanned the page. My heart stopped as I read the significant piece of information—12:30. The clock on the monitor read 12:05. I had fifteen minutes, or, rather, *we* had fifteen minutes. The heavy bag was slipping from my shoulder as I stuffed things into it. Where was the toddler? Grabbing his hand, the yogurt, which had mysteriously opened, flew from his grasp and splattered all over the floor. I couldn't stop. The volume from the stroller was gaining strength; our speed increased. Would we make it? Please, oh please!

42 *Comprehension Strategies*

These strategies are typically used before reading, during reading, and after reading. Each one has prompts or questions associated with it.

Predict –

- "Tell me what you think will happen in this story."
- "What do you think will happen next?"

Apply background knowledge –

- "Tell me what you know about (*fill in the blank with something from the reading selection*)."
- "Has this every happened to you?"

Retell –

- "Tell me all about what you just read."
- "Tell me two things that you learned from your reading."

Comprehension—*(circle one)* Listening or Reading

Student does this well: (circle)

predicts, applies background knowledge, retells

Student has difficulty with / I had to help the student with: